ALCATRAZ

Escape to the Wiregrass

Dale Cox & Rachael Cox

2025

ISBN:979-8-9927687-1-8

Library of Congress Control Number: 2025920056

DR Historic Preservation Inc
A 501(c)3 nonprofit organization
4520 Oak Grove Road
Bascom, Florida 32423

Remember them that are in bonds, as bound with them;
and them which suffer adversity, as being yourselves also in the body.
Hebrews: 13:3

This book is respectfully dedicated to
The Columbia Historical Society of Alabama,
And the men and women of
The Houston County Sheriff's Office.

Table of Contents

1.

The Bank of Columbia / 1

2.

Arrest and Return / 13

3.

The Rock / 27

4.

Escape / 37

5.

A Story from the Houston County Jail / 49

6.

Bank Robbery in Jay, Florida / 59

7.

The Robbery of Citizens State Bank in Marianna, Florida / 69

8.

The Death of Alfred Anglin / 79

9.

Mexico, the Bahamas, Brazil, and Colombia / 89

10.
Greenwood, Florida / 101

11.
The Chase comes to an End / 115

Photographs / 129

References / 159

More Books by Dale Cox / 165

Index / 167

Introduction

For decades, the legend of Alcatraz's most audacious escape has lingered, a tantalizing whisper in the fog-laden air of San Francisco Bay. Did they survive? Did Frank Morris and the Anglin brothers, John and Clarence, vanish into the currents, or did the unforgiving waters claim them? The mystery fueled speculation, fed conspiracy theories, and kept the story alive, a phantom ship sailing in the collective imagination.

Now, the fog lifts, and the truth, however bittersweet, emerges. This book is not a retelling of the escape itself; a narrative already etched into popular culture. Instead, it is the final chapter, a confirmation that the long-held question has found its answer. The surprising, yet inevitable, news has arrived: Frank Morris and John and Clarence Anglin, the men who dared to defy "The Rock," have all passed away.

Their deaths, however, do not close the book. They open it wider, revealing the intricate tapestry of their lives, both before and after the escape. We will journey back to the roots of their criminal careers, delving deep into the circumstances that led John and Clarence Anglin to Alcatraz. Specifically, we will examine the robbery of the Bank of Columbia, Alabama. This crime set them on a path culminating in the most infamous prison break in American history.

But the real heart of this narrative lies in the years after 1962. We will follow the elusive tracks of the escapees, tracing their potential movements, examining the scant evidence, and exploring the tantalizing possibilities. Where did they go? How did they survive? Did they build new lives, shrouded in anonymity, or did their past catch up with them?

1

This book will investigate potential additional crimes attributed to the escapees, examining the evidence with a critical eye. We will also explore the possibility of hidden lives, locations where they might have lived, and the people they might have encountered. We will sift through the rumors, the whispers, and the alleged sightings to separate fact from fiction, and to paint a more complete portrait of men who vanished into thin air.

This is not a romanticized tale of triumphant escape. It is a story of human fallibility, of the enduring power of hope, and of the inevitable passage of time. It is a journey into the shadows, a quest to understand the men behind the legend, and an effort to finally lay to rest the ghosts of Alcatraz.

ALCATRAZ
Escape to the Wiregrass

Chapter One

The Bank of Columbia

Against all odds, the three escapees of Alcatraz defied the unforgiving currents and reached the shores of freedom, surviving well into the 21st century. They existed in the shadows, their lives a constant dance with the ever-present threat of discovery by the FBI and US Marshals. Their escape, far from the idyllic vision they might have held, was a life of constant vigilance and, at times, unavoidable transgressions. Frank Lee Morris witnessed, from a distance, his story immortalized on the silver screen. Clint Eastwood portrayed him. However, the Anglin brothers, John and Clarence, carried a heavier burden: the haunting knowledge that their clandestine communication had indirectly led to the death of their brother, Alfred.

They witnessed the marvels of the 20th century, the impossible dream of humanity walking on the moon, yet John and Clarence were forever barred from the simple act of crossing their mother's threshold. Frank Morris was the first to succumb to time, passing away in 2008. Clarence followed in 2011, his life marked by hardship and the relentless toll of years spent in hiding. John William Anglin, the last of the trio, led a solitary existence, eventually reaching out to old friends and distant relatives in the Wiregrass region, which spans Southeast Alabama, Southwest Georgia, and Northwest Florida. These sporadic contacts, a

1

tenuous link to his past, persisted over the decades, only to abruptly cease in February 2024. At the age of 93, John William Anglin, the last living escapee of Alcatraz, finally surrendered to the inevitable, leaving behind a legacy shrouded in mystery and whispered legends.

They call it The Rock, even if it is named for pelicans. Alcatraz Island rises from San Francisco Bay like an ancient monster. The first Spanish explorers marveled at the hundreds of pelicans that covered the shores. It is a stark place today, even on sunny days. But when the cold and fog roll over the bay, Alcatraz Island becomes downright foreboding. This was America's original supermax prison. No one could escape. The water was too cold. There were sharks. Severe currents would carry what was left of you out to sea. And it was about as far from the sunshine and peanut fields of the Wiregrass region of Alabama, Georgia, and Florida as you could get. Yet the two places are linked by a remarkable story.

The escape from Alcatraz took place on the night of June 11-12, 1962. Frank Lee Morris and the brothers, Clarence Anglin and John William Anglin, cast off from the U.S. Penitentiary at Alcatraz Island, California, aboard a tiny inflatable raft of their construction. They wore homemade life preservers as an added safety measure. According to other prisoners who became suddenly talkative in the days that followed, their objective was nearby Angel Island, just over one mile away. Evidence linked to the escapees was found there over the coming days. The escape story, however, did not begin in San Francisco Bay. It began four and a half years earlier on a winter morning in the Wiregrass region of Southeast Alabama.

"At the time of the bank robbery, there was nothing historic about it, and it really didn't grab the attention of the public until after the escape from Alcatraz in 1962," says David Hunter of the Columbia Historical Society in Columbia, Alabama. He speaks of the society's headquarters and museum located in the historic Bank of Columbia building on South Main Street. "Two of the bank robbers, John and Clarence Anglin," he continues, "were two of the three escapees from Alcatraz." Even after that, according to Hunter, it was "very rare" for the news media to mention Columbia. Perhaps that is where the metro-focused press got it wrong.

2

John and Clarence Anglin were born in Seminole County, Georgia. It is a beautiful rural farm country – a place of fields, woods, rivers, and creeks. Although the boys were born in Donalsonville, the family lived just across the line in southern Miller County. Their home was in a small community between Colquitt and Donalsonville. Here, in neighboring Seminole and Early Counties in Southwest Georgia, they learned to swim, fish, hunt, and work for survival. They also spent time with relatives and friends across the Chattahoochee River in the thriving small town of Columbia, Alabama – a community that would remain in their minds for years to come.

Guy Anglin lives across the Chattahoochee River from Donalsonville in Jackson County, Florida. He spent the first years of his life in Colombia, where he went to school until 1951, "when my dad went broke farming and we moved to Polk County, Florida." He lived his teenage years in Auburndale, Florida, where his father was in the trucking business, and was attending college at Tampa in 1962 when he heard about the escape from Alcatraz:

> I was a student at the University of South Florida, and I came home one night, I think it was a Friday night or it may have been a Sunday night when I was getting ready to go back to Tampa, and there was a show called Armstrong Circle Theater and there was a special on there about the Alcatraz escape. That was really the first time I had ever known anything about Clarence and John.[1]

Years later, when he moved back to the Wiregrass area, he met a retired Methodist minister who knew John, Clarence, and Alfred in the years before they decided to pull off the bank heist at Columbia. "I went by there and introduced myself and the guy said, 'Oh, you're an Anglin?' and I said, 'Yeah'." It turned out that the minister had moved to Northwest Florida from Ruskin. In this Southwest Florida community, the parents of the three Anglin brothers settled after leaving the Wiregrass area.

---

[1] Guy Anglin, Interview with the author, February 21, 2018.

According to Guy Anglin's recollections, the clergyman recalled that the three future escapees "really weren't that bad" in their youth. He told the future U.S. Marine, U.S. Forest Service botanist, and noted conservationist that he "used to go by and pick them up and take them to church in the mornings." He also explained, possibly with a pastor's innocence, that law enforcement in Ruskin "started picking on" the three Anglin boys and "jailed them one time for something they hadn't done." The breaking point came when "one of them got involved with a young lady who wasn't a good influence." The minister summarized their early lives by telling Guy Anglin, "Of course, they never hurt anybody."[2]

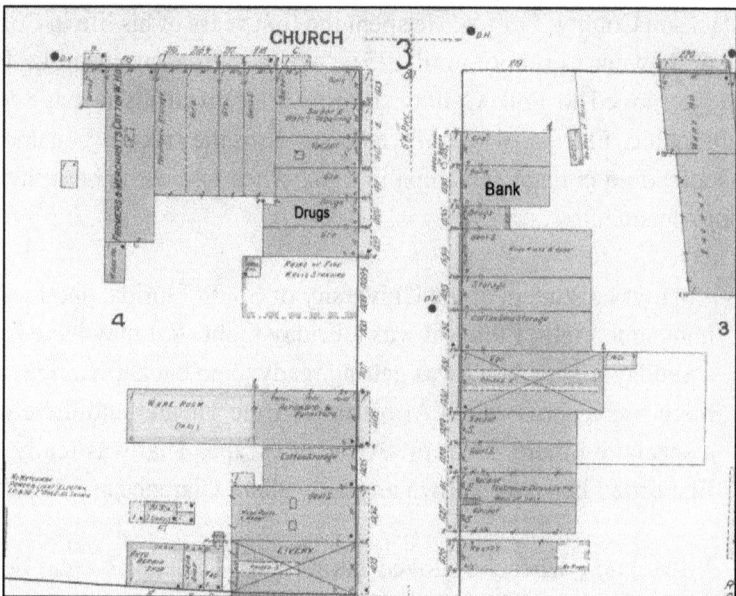

Map 1. The scene of the Bank of Columbia Robbery as shown on the 1916 Sanborn Fire Insurance Map for Columbia, Alabama. Witnesses heard the commotion from the bank building while at the drugstore across the street. The robbers fled east on Church. (LOC)

All three Anglin boys – Clarence, John, and Alfred – became involved in minor crimes and spent time behind bars. Clarence, for example, was the first to be sent to the Florida Industrial School for Boys (later known

---

[2] *Ibid.*

4

as Dozier School for Boys) in Marianna. He spent one year there before state authorities released him to his mother. Then came jail, followed by state prison. And not just in Florida. The family ranged as far north as Michigan, where farm work was available during the cherry harvest season. The boys learned their way around much of the United States. Their crimes were minor: breaking and entering, theft, escape. They were not particularly skilled at committing the crimes that landed them in prison, but they excelled at escaping – and they improved with each attempt. By 1958, all three were no longer kids, and all three had long histories with the law. That's when they decided that something bigger was in store for them. That's when they decided to go to Columbia.[3]

Columbia, Alabama, is a two-century-old town located just across the Chattahoochee River from the childhood territory of the Anglin boys in Miller, Seminole, and Early Counties, Georgia. It was a prosperous small community with a drug store, a grocery store, and a bank. It was the bank that brought the boys back home. "I wasn't aware of what was happening because I was in the drugstore, the Beasley Pharmacy, just across the way. Having a soda," says Dr. Adair Gilbert, PhD, a retired professor from Troy University. She was a teenage girl when she witnessed the Anglin brothers' robbery of the Bank of Columbia:

> I looked out and I saw things happening. Still, busy people coming and going around the bank was not unusual, until the bank president's wife Mrs. Florrie Oakley came into the little drugstore. She was just like this [demonstrating with both hands how Mrs. Oakley was shaking]; she was quivering. And she said, "They made me lay on the floor!" And I could not imagine Mrs. Florrie

---

[3] FBI, "Clarence Anglin, John William Anglin, and Frank Lee Morris," File Number 76-26295, Records of the Federal Bureau of Investigation, National Archives and Records Administration, College Park, MD, Photocopy in possession of the author.

ever being on the floor because she was such a prim and proper lady. So, it turns out that some guys had just robbed the bank.[4]

The bank targeted by the Anglin boys still stands in Columbia, Alabama. It is owned by the Columbia Historical Society, an organization dedicated to preserving not just the history of robbery but also that of an entire community. The structure is now a museum and was added to the National Register of Historic Places in 2024. Elliott Whitten of the society was among the society volunteers who assisted in developing a self-guided tour of Columbia. It includes the historic bank structure and other noteworthy sites now marked by interpretive panels throughout the town. He explains that visitors can pick up guide sheets from a kiosk next to the bank building and use them to tour the entire community.[5]

The boys showed patience and attention to detail in planning their crimes. They were in the area for several days, watching people who came and went. They set up a hideout as a base of operations on nearby Sowhatchee Creek, a tributary of the Chattahoochee River, located due east of Columbia in Early County, Georgia. From there, they were able to study the local road network and plan the best escape routes. The Anglin boys also came and went to and from Columbia at will, refreshing their memories of the community and observing changes that had taken place since their boyhood days. "They used to spend some summers in Columbia," says Clint Smith, another member of the Columbia Historical Society, "so they were very familiar with the town." His friends included now-deceased individuals who knew the Anglin brothers well. "They had a relative here, and when they were boys, they would come over and spend time in Columbia." According to Smith, another individual who knew the brothers was former Columbia mayor James Green, "[He] used to go fishing with them, palling around with them, swimming at the swimming hole, and so forth, so they were familiar with the little town. And they

---

[4] Adair Gilbert, PhD, Interview with the author, March 3, 2018.
[5] Eliott Whitten, Columbia Historical Society, Interview with the author, March 3, 2018.

probably heard rumors that the bank was full of money and that we had one policeman. It makes sense that maybe that's why they selected Columbia."[6]

There is also a persistent rumor in the area that a relative of the boys deposited a large sum of money – the proceeds from the year's peanut harvest – at the Bank of Columbia on the morning of the robbery. There is no way to confirm this story. Everyone at the bank that day is now deceased, the bank records are inaccessible, and the Anglin brothers are not talking! If true, however, this would be a powerful motive. Most of the farms in the area grew peanuts as their primary cash crop at the time. Nearby, Dothan was and is the "Peanut Capital of the World." The bulk of a farmer's income typically comes in the fall, when they complete their peanut harvest. If Clarence, John, and Alfred knew that a relative had a large sum of cash and was planning to deposit it in Columbia, they might consider it a juicy target for robbery. They could also do so in good conscience, since they would be stealing from the bank, not their relative, in their way of thinking.[7]

Whatever the truth of the peanut money story, the boys chose their escape route and finalized their plans. The Columbia bank job would be their biggest crime yet, and they had done all they could to ensure it turned out right. As they slipped away from their hideout at Sowhatchee Creek, they knew they were playing a dangerous game. The payoff, however, could be huge.

The Bank of Columbia robbery occurred on the morning of January 17, 1958. It was a Friday:

> According to old newspaper articles, it happened at 10 a.m. that morning, and the three Anglin brothers walked through the front door – unmasked, not trying to hide their identities – and

---

[6] Clint Smith, Columbia Historical Society, Interview with the author, June 1, 2018.

[7] Story commonly told in Seminole, Jackson, and Houston Counties in the 1970s and 1980s.

proceeded to rob the Bank of Columbia. Luckily, there were no customers in the bank at that time. There were just three bank employees – the bank president and his wife, who was also the secretary, and Mr. C.L. Williams, the teller. The three robbers and the three employees were the only people in the bank during the holdup.[8]

Family members of Bank President Mr. Walter F. Oakley, Jr., recall how they first heard about the robbery. Ben Oakley, a nephew, remembers, for example, that he was traveling at the time and headed back to his office in Dothan:

I decided to stop by my grandmother's house here in Columbia, and we were sitting in the den talking when my Uncle Marion came up to the house and said the bank had been robbed. My Uncle Walter was president of the bank at the time. I did not go down to the bank because they had people in – police and FBI and all of that – at the time, hunting for the people that had robbed the bank.[9]

Historian David Hunter has spent years researching what happened inside the bank building that day. "They tied up Mr. Oakley and forced him at gunpoint to stand in the corner," he indicates, "and the other two employees were made to lie down on the floor." He also makes clear that the threat of violence was very real: "And their lives were threatened if they did not cooperate."[10]

One of the Anglins pointed what appeared to the employees to be a massive gun directly into their faces. When the FBI asked teller C.L. Williams about the weapon, he responded that he didn't "really know what size it was, all I can tell you is you could stick your fist down the barrel

[8] David Hunter, Historian, Columbia Historical Society, Interview with the author, February 1, 2018.
[9] Ben Oakley, Interview with the author, June 6, 2018.
[10] Hunter, interview.

that far!" – indicating a point halfway up his forearm. Dr. Adair Gilbert also heard the same story from Mr. Williams, who told her that the weapon used by the Anglin brothers "looked like a cannon." Many, including members of the Anglin family, believe that the gun used in the robbery was a toy gun. They say that the three brothers thought that they could not be charged with armed robbery if they did not use a real firearm in the commission of the crime. An Alabama state patrolman in 1962 told newspaper reporters that two of the robbers were armed with snub-nosed .38 caliber revolvers.[11]

Questions about the guns aside, the robbers were forceful in their treatment of the employees, especially bank president Walter F. Oakley, Jr. After making teller C.L. Williams and Mrs. Oakley get down on the floor, "They put a clothes hanger around his neck and was kind of choking him and making him go where they wanted him to go," said his nephew, Ben Oakley. Mr. Oakley told authorities that he "almost screamed" when one of the armed men confronted him outside his office and told him, "I'll kill you." After collecting all the cash they could find, the robbers forced the three employees into a rear office and told them to stay there. While the frightened bank workers waited to learn their fates, the three Anglin brothers headed for the door. [12]

As they crossed the mosaic that typically welcomed customers to the Bank of Columbia, they received the unwitting help of a local citizen. Jimmy Nix, the son of a local grocer, offered a bit of Southern hospitality by holding open the door for the three so they could pass through before him. Clint Smith often tells the story about his long-time friend's brush with American crime history:

> He was working with his dad in the grocery store directly across the street – Nix's Grocery – and one of his tasks was to get the cash in a canvas bag and make deposits in the bank. So, Jimmy was walking across the street to the bank, and he told me several

---

[11] Oakley, interview; Gilbert, interview; *Birmingham News*, January 18, 1958.
[12] Oakley, interview; *Birmingham News*, January 18, 1958.

times that when he got there, he saw someone coming out of the door, so he held the door open for them. He stood back like a kid with good manners would do and these three men came out, got in the car, and drove away in a big hurry. And Jimmy realized later they were the bank robbers. On the next day, Jimmy was interviewed by some FBI agents. They asked him about the men. He described them best, which probably wasn't very good. As a result of that, Jimmy expressed to some other friends some fear that he would be on a hit list because he was revealing the bank robbers' identities. He didn't know who they were, but he said what they looked like.[13]

Across the street, a then-teenaged Adair Gilbert watched as the men made their getaway. Newspapers quoted Mr. Oakley as saying that the employees remained in the back office "only about two or three minutes before we got out and spread the alarm." Gilbert distinctly remembered how Mrs. Oakley came running out to spread the news:

> ...[S]he had come across the street, and he didn't make it across the street. He fainted before he could get across the street from all the excitement. You know, everything was just all of a sudden abuzz, and cars, and people running in and out. And the police showed up, or some law enforcement showed up and chased these guys, and as I understood, they chased them across the river towards Georgia.[14]

John Beasley was also on the scene that morning. He was the new owner of the half-century-old drugstore directly across the street from the Bank of Columbia. This was the same pharmacy where future business professor Dr. Adair Gilbert, a teenage girl, was enjoying a soda. Beasley

---

[13] Smith, interview.
[14] Gilbert, interview.

remembered that he was sitting at a table in the same soda fountain area, discussing an order with a drug salesperson when the robbery took place:

> Back then, we had a soda fountain in the drugstore, had soda fountain tables back there where people could sit around and drink their malts and Cokes and Pepsis and whatever. That particular day, that morning, I had a drug salesman, Mr. Robert Reddon from Headland, who worked for Southeastern Drug Company, and he and I were back there. . . Mr. Reddon and I were sitting at one of the soda fountain tables, and I don't know exactly what time it was, when we heard a clamoring noise and a person hollering loudly. We walked to the front of the drugstore. Mr. Walter F. Oakley, Jr., who was president of the bank, came out on the sidewalk. When we got to the front of the drugstore and looked across and opened the door, he was yelling, "We've been cleaned out!" "We've been cleaned out!" And then he fainted on the sidewalk. Right there in front of the bank, there.[15]

The outlaws fled east across the Chattahoochee River into Georgia, following a preplanned route. The Bank of Columbia robbery was over almost before anyone in town knew it had happened. To John Beasley, it was a "very exciting day, it was a scary day." He remembered that few people saw the getaway car, and those who did were unaware of its significance. As a result, they did not remember enough details to provide much help to law enforcement. When the FBI and other authorities started interviewing residents in search of clues, there was very little information to be had. More than sixty years later, Beasley voiced the question that many in the community still ask, "Why would anybody pick a little town like Columbia to rob the bank?"

Details of the escape gradually became apparent as investigators sought to uncover the facts of the robbery. After crossing the Chattahoochee River bridge into Georgia with no police car in pursuit, the

---

[15] John Beasley, Interview with the author, September 9, 2018.

three Anglin brothers returned to their hideout on Sowhatchee Creek. Why they went back there is a mystery to this day. Was someone else waiting there for them? Was a fourth party involved in the robbery? From Sowhatchee Creek, they headed south to Blountstown, Florida. There, Alfred Anglin took a bus to Bainbridge in Decatur County, Georgia, where he recovered the second car that the men had brought north from Tampa and left stashed at a hotel. Clarence and John, meanwhile, drove straight south from Blountstown to Tampa, where Alfred soon linked up with them. Back together again, the three men suddenly turned back north, determined to leave the Southeast. By employing this bizarre escape path, they managed to escape the Columbia area before law enforcement could catch them. It helped that eyewitnesses seemed confused over exactly what types of cars they were driving and which way they were headed.

Some people thought they were driving a dark Chevrolet. Others were certain that they were in 1957 Cadillacs – one of them light blue with South Carolina plates. Most had seen them leave the bank and turn east, heading for the Chattahoochee River bridge into Georgia. Others were equally convinced – and remain so – that they turned west, passing Columbia High School as they raced toward Dothan. Roadblocks were set up in all directions, but the suspects managed to slip through the fingers of law enforcement in Alabama, Georgia, and Florida. Legendary Sheriff Lamar Hadden of Houston County, Alabama, then a deputy, told one of his future deputies many years later that "we missed them by minutes."[16]

Something, however, went wrong with the Anglin brothers' plan. Investigators quickly developed information that they were behind the robbery. "It was strange," remembered Ben Oakley, "the FBI – when they got to talking about where they had been, one of the men with the FBI seemed to know something about the Anglins." Agents quickly found the brothers' trail and followed it north across the eastern United States to Ohio.[17]

---

[16] Oakley, interview; *Birmingham News*, January 18, 1958; Sheriff Donald Valenza, Houston County, Alabama, Personal Communication, November 2024.
[17] Oakley, interview.

Chapter Two

Arrest and Return

FLEEING THE CHAOS THEY UNLEASHED in Columbia, Alabama, the Anglin brothers sought refuge in Ohio. Their destination felt impossibly distant, a psychological chasm as vast as one million miles. Yet, even one million literal miles would not have sufficed to outrun the relentless pursuit of justice. The determination to apprehend them and return them to Houston County was unwavering.

The discovery of their abandoned getaway car, a black vehicle found near Sowhatchee Creek in Early County, provided a crucial lead. It rapidly focused the Federal Bureau of Investigation's attention on Alfred, John William, and Clarence Anglin as the prime suspects in the Bank of Columbia robbery. They were well-known figures in the town, whose presence was observed and remembered. Multiple residents had seen them loitering on a bench opposite the bank in the days leading up to the heist. Furthermore, their visits to a relative on the south side of town were relayed to investigators, providing further confirmation of their involvement.

These tips quickly propelled law enforcement onto their trail. Subsequent inquiries into their associates revealed that John Anglin maintained a relationship with a woman in Hamilton, Ohio, a town situated approximately twenty miles north of Cincinnati. This critical piece of information allowed FBI agents to anticipate the Anglins' destination almost as swiftly as the fugitives themselves. Within a mere five days, the crime was effectively solved, the net tightening around the brothers as they sought to disappear into the anonymity of the north. Seven FBI agents raided two houses in Hamilton on the morning of January 22, 1958, arresting all three of the Anglin brothers. The *Cincinnati Enquirer* reported the next day that agents found Alfred and his wife, 15-year-old Janet Anglin, "sleeping, and prodded them awake with machine guns." Also seized were Fern Taylor, age 60, and his daughter Helen Taylor McIntosh, age 32. Helen, a married woman, was reportedly estranged from her husband. Several sources named her as the girlfriend of John Anglin. Mr. Taylor and the two women were charged as accessories after the fact to the robbery of the Bank of Columbia. Bonds for Helen Taylor McIntosh and Janet Anglin were set at $5,000 each, while Fern Taylor's was set at $10,000. All faced serious prison time, which would weigh heavily on Alfred and John Anglin.[18]

FBI agents also recovered the bulk of the money from the Alabama robbery. $13,648.38 in cash was found in the two homes raided by the FBI, along with $5,000 in travelers' checks. Among the three vehicles the Bureau took was a "small, fast sports car." Two guns and "drilling equipment" were found as well. The guns were not toys. Bond for the three brothers was set at $20,000, but even if they had been able to pay it, Clarence and Alfred would not have been going anywhere, since they were also under hold as escapees from a state prison in Florida.[19]

The origin of the $5,000 in travelers' checks possessed by the Anglins is no mystery. They had converted part of their cash loot into a more secure currency. That the men might possess that much in traveler's checks instead of cash might seem odd in today's world of credit and debit cards. Although credit cards were invented in 1946, they did not gain widespread popularity in the United States until the 1970s and 1980s. Even then, they

---

[18] *The Journal Herald*, January 23, 1958; *Cincinnati Enquirer*, January 23, 1958.

[19] *Ibid.*; *Cincinnati Enquirer*, January 22, 1958, 4.

would not have been the first choice of bank robbers due to the inconvenience of travel. Travelers' checks, if the reader is unfamiliar with them, are still in use. Before the advent of credit cards, however, many Americans commonly used them to cover expenses while traveling. Sizeable national bank chains were not as standard as they are today, but traveler's checks could be used to pay for lodging, food, and other expenses. Almost any bank would cash them, and they were insured. Unlike cash, you never lost their value even if they were lost or stolen. By purchasing travelers' checks, the Anglins could travel safely without flashing large sums of cash.

It is unclear whether Clarence, John, and Alfred Anglin, or their friends fully understood the case against them. The Gideon v. Wainwright case, which guaranteed the right to an attorney in criminal cases, was not decided by the U.S. Supreme Court until 1963. When the Anglins were arrested in 1958, they had no right to an attorney if they could not afford one. It is not immediately clear whether they had independent legal counsel when they made their decisions during the days and weeks following their arrest. The charges against them were more complicated than they likely realized and led to far more serious incarceration than they probably anticipated.

On the day of their arrest, it appears that John, Clarence, and Alfred at least resisted the idea of entering a plea to the bank robbery in Alabama. Awakened by FBI agents pointing the muzzles of machine guns at their faces, they had been rousted from their beds with no time to discuss things with either each other or their compatriots. John's 15-year-old wife, Alfred's married girlfriend, and her father, Fern Taylor, were also in custody. The severity of the three men's interrogations and the information they were given about the three alleged accessories all factored into their decision-making. They did not want to return to Alabama to face trial, and that was undoubtedly part of their reasoning as they each considered the situation that day. None of them likely considered or even knew that they could also face state charges in Alabama, as well as federal charges against them in Ohio. What the Assistant U.S. Attorney in Cincinnati told them is not known. Still, reporters there believed that the Anglins were led to believe that they were assured that a guilty plea by the men in Ohio meant they would not be going back to Alabama. The *Cincinnati Enquirer* reported that this was a factor in their decision to change their plea to guilty. "The three Anglin brothers, awaiting prosecution for a $19,000 Alabama bank robbery, changed their minds yesterday and decided to enter a plea in Cincinnati rather than be returned to Alabama."[20]

The deal undoubtedly was an agreement that freed Fern Taylor, Helen Taylor McIntosh, and Janet Anglin as well. The three were released, and the charges against them were dropped. Despite what the newspaper was told and the men believed, however, the three Anglin brothers were still heading back to Alabama. The long arm of the law was reaching out for them, and it would not be satisfied until they stood before a judge and jury in a Houston County courtroom.

Within three weeks of their arrest, Clarence, John, and Alfred Anglin appeared before U.S. District Judge Frank M. Johnson in Montgomery, Alabama. They signed documents waiving their rights to have the evidence against them presented to a federal grand jury and to have their case heard by a jury of their peers. Their guilty pleas were repeated to Judge Johnson on February 10, 1958. Clarence and Alfred, who authorities believed were carrying handguns during the robbery, received 15 years in federal prison. John, who was not armed, received 10 years. From Montgomery, they were transported to the U.S. Penitentiary in Atlanta to begin serving their sentences. They recognized acquaintances there and settled into a well-known routine to all three - the daily grind of "standing time." The Anglins undoubtedly thought that their ordeal of FBI agents, courtrooms, and uncertainty about the future was over for the time being. Unknown to the three men, however, legal wheels were turning to bring them back to Alabama even as they arrived in Atlanta.[21]

Circuit Solicitor Forrest Adams of Houston County wanted to try the Anglin brothers in a Dothan courtroom. The robbery of more than $13,000

---

[20] *Cincinnati Enquirer*, January 25, 1958.
[21] *The Dothan Eagle*, March 16, 1958.

16

was no small thing in Houston County, and Adams was determined to see that the men faced state charges in addition to the federal charges on which they entered their guilty pleas. He faced a problem, however, because the three convicted outlaws were now serving time in a U.S. prison, and he was not even presenting evidence yet to a grand jury in Dothan. There was no state indictment against the Anglins, so they faced no state charges. For Solicitor Adams to get the Anglin brothers back to Alabama, he first had to charge them with something.

Fortunately for him – and unfortunately for the three brothers – this process was already underway. Summons had been issued on January 30 for key witnesses in the case to appear before the Grand Jury for the Circuit Court of Houston County on February 12, 1958. Among those seen entering the courtroom while the grand jury was in session were Bank of Columbia President Walter F. Oakley, Mrs. Walter F. Oakley, and bank teller C.L. Williams, Jr. What they told the grand jury was kept confidential per state law in Alabama, but they undoubtedly described what they each saw and experienced on the morning of January 17, 1958. It was enough and the grand jurors returned a joint indictment against John William Anglin, Alfred Ray Anglin, and Clarence Anglin for robbery.

The February 1958 indictment by the grand jury in Houston County— which conducted its proceedings entirely after the three men entered their pleas in federal court, were sentenced, and started serving their time in federal prison—gave Solicitor Forrest Adams the legal ammunition he needed to get the men back to the county. Now, he just had to figure out how to pry them away from the hands of the U.S. government.

In the end, he conceived a then-novel legal maneuver. Instead of issuing a normal subpoena or trying to request custody of the men from U.S. Bureau of Prisons authorities, Adams turned to a concept that some legal scholars say had not been used in Alabama since the Reconstruction Era. He filed a motion asking Houston County Circuit Judge Keener Baxley to issue a writ of *habeas corpus ad prosequendum* against the Marshal of the United States District Court, Middle District of Alabama, as well as the warden of the United States Penitentiary at Atlanta, Georgia. Writs of *habeas corpus ad prosequendum* are not particularly rare. They are often used when parties in the federal courts need to retrieve an inmate from a county jail or state prison to give testimony. However, for a county to use the process the other way around in 1958 was another matter. What gave the process teeth in the case of the Anglins was that the U.S. Marshal Charles S. Prescott was assigned to the court in Montgomery, Alabama. This placed him within reach of state authorities. Warden Fred T. Wilkinson in Atlanta was another matter, but Solicitor Adams only needed one of the two.

Judge Baxley received the requested writ on February 28, 1958. It informed the two federal authorities that John William Anglin, Alfred Ray Anglin, and Clarence Anglin were confined in the Federal Penitentiary at Atlanta, Georgia and that the Grand Jury of Houston County had returned a joint indictment against them for robbery. A copy of the indictment was attached. The writ went on to state that arraignment for the three men was set for Monday, March 10, 1958, with their trial scheduled to begin on Friday, March 14. Under the writ, Prescott and Wilkinson were directed to bring the three Anglin men before Judge Baxley in the Houston County Courthouse at 9 a.m. on March 10. The writ was approved by the judge on the day that it was filed. Roy Hill, the Clerk of the Circuit Court for Houston County, prepared certified copies for the Sheriff's Office to serve on Marshal Prescott and Wardon Wilkinson.

The Anglins began their unexpected journey back to Houston County on March 3, 1958. Deputy U.S. Marshal Jack S. Johnson in Montgomery accepted service of the writ of *habeas corpus ad prosequendum* requiring that the three men be brought before Judge Keener Baxley. He executed the writ on Warden Fred T. Wilkson at the U.S. Penitentiary in Atlanta on March 9, taking John, Clarence, and Alfred into custody for the trip to Dothan. As required, he appeared with them at the Houston County Courthouse on the morning of March 10, 1958:

The three Anglin brothers, Alfred, Clarence and John, were arraigned here today on armed robbery charges in connection with the Jan. 17 Bank of Columbia holdup and Circuit Judge Keener Baxley set their trials for Friday.

The men, all under heavy federal sentences after pleading guilty to bank robbery charges, were brought here quietly last night under heavy guard. They will remain in federal custody while here.

If convicted here, they could receive the death sentence but Solicitor Forrest Adams said they must complete federal prison terms before beginning any state sentences they might be given.[22]

The mention of possible death sentences in the *Dothan Eagle's* coverage of the arraignment may explain why the Anglin brothers were so anxious to avoid trial in Houston County. Another apparent reason is that a second trial would mean more prison time for them.

The newspaper also provided some detail on the legal maneuvering that led to the return of the now-convicted bank robbers to Houston County:

In obtaining custody of the Anglins for trial, Adams applied for a writ of habeas corpus ad prosequendum, which calls for the return of the suspects to the jurisdiction in which the crime was committed. It was issued by Judge Baxley.

Adams explained that the federal charge of bank robbery is separate from the armed robbery charge for which they will stand trial here.

Judge Baxley said he could find no record of such change in custody in Alabama since post-Civil War days

---

[22] Ken Hogg, "Anglins Brought Here To Face Circuit Trial, *Dothan Eagle*, March 10, 1958.

when prisoners were shifted from one jurisdiction to another.[23]

Now securely in Houston County awaiting trial, which was set to take place in short order – just four days after their arraignment – the Anglin brothers spent their time in the historic old county jail on North Oates Street in downtown Dothan, which still stands as of today. They never left the custody of the U.S. Marshals Service during their five days in the city.

The joint trial of the three bank robbers for armed robbery convened on Friday morning, March 14, 1958. Things began with a strange twist. C.L. Williams, Jr., the bank cashier subpoenaed to testify as a witness against the Anglins, was also present as a member of the pool of potential jurors for the case. The reason for this error occurring when the juror summonses were mailed out is unclear. 1958 was before the days of computer mailings. Regardless, Judge Baxley excused Williams from the jury. It is unclear whether he had contact with other prospective jurors or if the defense objected that his presence might have prejudiced the entire jury pool.[24]

The defense tried to stop the entire trial on constitutional grounds. After the arraignment of the Anglin brothers that Monday, Dothan attorneys H.K. and James F. Martin stepped forward to represent them. They tried to amend the not-guilty pleas that all three brothers entered independently, urging the court to stop the proceeding. Filed on Tuesday morning, March 11, the plea amendment noted that John, Clarence, and Alfred Anglin had once been in jeopardy for the crimes for which they were now indicted in Houston County and that they had already been arraigned and entered guilty pleas in the United States District Court for the Middle District of Alabama for those crimes. The two Martins argued that there was no real difference between the crimes for which the U.S.

---

[23] *Ibid.*

[24] Ken Hogg, "Bank Bandit Brother Trio Put On Trial," *Dothan Eagle*, March 14, 1958.

Attorney charged the Anglin brothers and those they now faced in Houston County.

The attempt to invoke the U.S. Constitution's protection against double jeopardy failed:

> Circuit Judge Keener Baxley ordered the double jeopardy plea stricken after a hearing before the trial started.
>
> The defense counsel, H.K. and J.F. Martin, claim the Anglins were being prosecuted for a crime for which they have already been sentenced in U.S. Court.
>
> Solicitor Forrest Adams, however, produced legal books which stated flatly that Federal offenses and state offenses were of a different nature.
>
> The Anglins were brought into court shortly after 9 a.m. without their shackles.[25]

For the last time in their lives, the Anglin brothers faced a trial before a jury of their peers. The indictment consisted of four counts:

1. That John William Anglin, Clarence Anglin, and Alfred Ray Anglin took $18,911.65 from the Bank of Columbia against the will of Walter F. Oakley by violence to his person or by putting him in such fear that he unwillingly parted with the money.
2. That the three men took the money from the bank against the will of Florrie Oakley by violence to her person or by putting her in such fear that she unwillingly parted with it.
3. The Anglin brothers took the money from the bank against C.L. Williams, Jr.'s will by violence to his

---

[25] *Ibid.*

person or putting him in such fear that he parted with
it.

4. That the three men stole $18,911.64 from Walter F.
    Oakley against his will by violence to his person or
    by putting him in such fear that he unwillingly parted
    with it.

The fourth of these charges stemmed from the fact that Mr. Oakley
was the bank's owner and personally liable for the deposits, despite the
FDIC's insurance coverage.

Testimony in the case began as solicitor Adams called bank cashier
C.L. Williams, Jr., to the stand. Williams testified that he was at the teller's
window on the morning of January 17, 1958, when Clarence and John
Anglin approached and asked him to give them change for a $5 bill. At
this point, Alfred entered the teller's cage with a gun pulled and told the
cashier to "get on the floor." Williams did not immediately comply, but
Clarence now put a hand on a gun in his belt that had not been showing
before. The bank employee began to get down as ordered, but his
movements were too slow to satisfy Alfred, who struck him across the
neck to expedite the process.[26]

Mr. Williams went on to describe the actions of the three robbery
suspects from that point:

> Alfred Anglin ransacked drawers in the cashier's
> counter, emptying the contents in a large sack. After an
> unsuccessful search for additional money, he ordered
> Williams and Mrs. Walter Oakley, the bookkeeper, to an
> office in the rear of the building.
>
> Clarence Anglin was already in the office holding
> bank President Walter Oakley at gunpoint. Oakley's
> hands had been tied behind his back.

---

[26] *Ibid.*

Alfred entered the rear office and ordered Oakley to go to the front of the building and open the vault, but Oakley replied that he could not do so because his hands were tied.

Alfred then ordered Williams to open the vault, and Williams did so. Williams later returned to the office, where he, Oakley, and Mrs. Oakley were held at gunpoint by Clarence.[27]

Clarence Anglin finally left the three employees alone in the bank building's back room, ordering them to remain there "until we have gotten away."

Mrs. Oakley's testimony did not vary significantly from that of Mr. Williams, although she did mention trying to close the outer door of the vault. She described how Alfred Anglin warned her that "if you do that again, I'll blow your head off." Unlike Williams, she never saw John Anglin during the robbery.

Walter F. Oakley, the bank president, took the stand when the jury returned from lunch and gave his version of the robbery. Like the story told by his wife, his version of events also did not differ significantly from the narrative presented to the jury by C.L. Williams, Jr. He described how Clarence Anglin forced him into the back room of the bank and tied his hands behind his back. He also said that he was afraid for his life and that he saw both Clarence and Alfred carrying handguns during the robbery.

The final witness for the prosecution was FBI Agent John Lill. He gave jurors a summary of his agency's investigation of the robbery:

The Anglins left Tampa, Fla., on Jan. 15 in two automobiles and went to Bainbridge, Ga., where they registered at a motel on U.S. Highway 84 west of town.

---

[27] *Ibid.*

23

They spent the following day riding along the roads in the Georgia area. After changing automobiles on the second day, they drove to Columbia.

Alfred Anglin entered the town after leaving John and Clarence on the outskirts. At the bank, he asked for penny wrappers while looking over the interior.

The Anglins returned in a unit later and committed the robbery, leaving Georgia on State Highway 62 and turning right on a paved road about three miles inside the state.

At Blountstown, Fla., Alfred caught a bus to Bainbridge for the second automobile, and the others continued to Tampa. The bank's money was split when Alfred arrived in Tampa.

After a day or two in Tampa, the three went to Hamilton, Ohio, where they were arrested.[28]

The Anglin brothers did not take the stand in their defense, and jurors took only one hour to find all three guilty of robbery under the laws of the State of Alabama. Sentenced to 25 years each, the three men were returned to the U.S. Penitentiary in Atlanta by the U.S. Marshals, who still had them in custody. Judge Baxley was not immediately sure whether the sentences would run consecutively or concurrently. It was ultimately determined that they would run concurrently, thereby adding 10 years to the prison terms of Clarence and Alfred Anglins. In comparison, John Anglin would serve an additional 15 years in state prison upon the completion of his shorter federal prison sentence.

Houston County and the State of Alabama had exacted their measure of justice for the robbery of the Bank of Columbia. However, authorities in Dothan and Columbia had no way of knowing that their victory was to be short-lived or that they would soon find their names intertwined in the

---

[28] *Ibid.*

history of America's best-known prison escape. History, however, has a surprising way of involving those who least expect it.

Chapter Three

The Rock

THE ANGLIN BROTHERS FOUND THEMSELVES back in Atlanta, where fate intervened in the form of an old acquaintance from their time at Florida State Prison in Raiford: Frank Lee Morris. Morris's criminal record surpassed their own, marked by more severe offenses. Beyond bank burglary, he was entangled in multiple drug-related arrests. Before long, their minds turned to the topic favored in the dreams of many inmates. They started plotting to escape, but this time the system was ahead of them. The discovery of meticulously crafted escape plans within the Atlanta facility triggered a swift response from federal authorities. Clarence and John Anglin were transferred to the U.S. Penitentiary in Leavenworth, Kansas, while Alfred remained behind, their paths diverging permanently. Despite their efforts, they would never see him again. The brothers' penchant for escape persisted in Leavenworth, with at least two attempts, including Clarence's audacious plan to conceal himself within a large breadbox. Exasperated by their persistent escape attempts, prison authorities made the decisive move to transfer John and Clarence to the infamous Alcatraz.

The U.S. Penitentiary on Alcatraz Island was called "The Rock" for a reason. So far as anyone knew, no inmate had ever escaped from the prison. The water of San Francisco Bay is cold, the currents are treacherous, and it is a long way to shore. Guards at the prison told inmates that sharks swarmed in the bay, but this was a psychological tactic used to make the water look even more intimidating. Sharks are not a particular threat to humans around Alcatraz Island.

The prison itself had a long history when John and Clarence Anglin arrived. Alcatraz Island was reserved for government purposes by order of President Millard Fillmore in 1850. Four years after the first federal installation on the island, a lighthouse began operation. It was, in fact, the first lighthouse on the entire Pacific coast of the United States. The real intent of the U.S., however, was to use the island as part of a triangular defense of the entrance to San Francisco Bay. Military engineers viewed the rocky natural topography of Alcatraz with awe and conceived a design for a massive fortification built into the rocky bluffs. Work started in 1853, and the fort was occupied by its garrison in 1859. It mounted 111 cannons.[29]

The fortress never came under fire during the Civil War, but it did serve a different purpose as a prison throughout its military life. From when regular troops first arrived on the island in 1859 until they left in 1933, there were always at least some prisoners there. A temporary prison facility was built to confine "disloyal citizens" and others during the Civil War. Among these was the Chairman of the California Democratic Committee, who gave a speech during the 1864 Presidential campaign that Republicans did not like. He was not released until he posted a bond and took an oath of allegiance to the Union.[30]

The type of prisoners held at Alcatraz expanded in the 1870s to include American Indian chiefs and warriors who surrendered to or were captured by U.S. troops during the wars of conquest across the West. These included Modoc, Paiute, Apache, Hopi, and others. The use of the island

---

[29] National Park Service, "The Post on Alcatraces," National Park Service, last modified December 2, 2019, accessed September 1, 2024, https://www.nps.gov/alca/learn/historyculture/the-post-on-alcatraces.htm.
[30] *Ibid.*

to house Native American prisoners left a wound that remains with many American Indians today.

The number of military prisoners at Alcatraz expanded rapidly when the nation engaged in the Spanish-American War. By 1900, 441 men were held in the facility, which had grown to include Upper and Lower Prisons. These structures were made of wood, which was not the ideal material for use in building confinement facilities, as some of the prisoners were arsonists and attempted to burn the buildings down. The 1906 San Francisco Earthquake added to the message when a resulting firestorm swept through the city and almost reached the jail where 176 inmates were held. Those inmates were temporarily moved to Alcatraz.[31]

The U.S. Government recognized that the island's future was as a prison and not as a defensive point. Hence, it turned to constructing impressive concrete facilities and barracks. The facility was redesignated as the Pacific Branch, U.S. Military Prison, Alcatraz Island. A new cell house included 600 cells. It is interesting to note that during its early 20th-century military years, Alcatraz was a minimum-security prison. The inmates were only locked up at night. They spent their days working, attending class, or enjoying recreation. Some even served as babysitters for the families of army officers at the Presidio and Fort Point.[32]

Supply and other issues led the military to close the facility on Alcatraz Island in 1933. Most prisoners were transferred to different prisons, but 32 of the most intractable were handed over to the U.S. Bureau of Prisons. The Bureau took over the facility, over the objections of many San Francisco citizens who did not want a central prison in the middle of their bay, and started to bring in some of the worst criminals in American history. Al Capone, "Machine Gun" Kelly, "Bumpy" Johnson, "Doc" Barker, Mickey Cohen, "Creepy" Karpis, and "Whitey" Bulger all served time on the Rock. And so did bank robbers named Anglin from Florida, and Morris, from Louisiana.

---

[31] *Ibid.*
[32] *Ibid.*

Frank, Inmate Number AZ1441, arrived at Alcatraz on January 29, 1960, after briefly escaping the Louisiana State Penitentiary, where he served a 10-year sentence for bank burglary. John Anglin, Inmate Number AZ 1476, came through intake at the island nine months later, on October 24, 1960. Clarence was not far behind, arriving at Alcatraz as Inmate Number AZ 1485 on January 16, 1961. About four years had passed since he and his brothers robbed the Bank of Columbia.[33]

Surprisingly, the two Anglin brothers and Morris found themselves in nearby cells along the same corridor. Someone at the prison may have tried to show a small measure of compassion by putting Clarence next to his brother John when he arrived at the notorious prison. It was a kind thing to do. It also dramatically increased the odds that the two would cooperate on an escape plan. So did putting them so close to their acquaintance Frank Lee Morris, whose intelligence scored in the top 2% of the prison's population.[34]

Morris and the Anglins were preoccupied with escaping, perhaps even more so than most other inmates. Guards and intake officers' assertions that Alcatraz was "escape-proof" likely piqued their interest, and it probably did not take long for them to hear the legend of Ted Cole and Ralph Roe. The two men were convicted bank robbers from Oklahoma, but more than that, they were criminals from the word go. One Oklahoma sheriff said Cole was "more trouble than all the other prisoners we ever had." Roe, meanwhile, was part of the notorious Underhill gang of robbers and murderers. The men were noted for their sometimes-violent escape attempts and had arrived in San Francisco for confinement on Alcatraz aboard the same train.[35]

Even before reaching the island prison in California, the 24-year-old Theodore "Ted" Cole did not expect to like it there. U.S. District Judge Edgar S. Vaught sentenced him to 50 years on the Rock for

---

[33] FBI, "Clarence Anglin," file no. 76-26295.
[34] Robert D. McFadden, "Anniversary of a Mystery at Alcatraz," *The New York Times*, June 9, 2012.
[35] *Dallas Morning News*, December 17, 1937.

kidnapping a pipeline worker named J.A. Rutherford in Cushing, Oklahoma. Cole forced Rutherford to drive him to Dallas. When Vaught handed down his sentence, Cole told fellow inmates that he did not think he would like Alcatraz and probably would not stay long enough to become bored.[36]

Cole and Roe left Alcatraz between 1 and 1:30 p.m. on December 16, 1937. Whether they had fabricated a raft or life preservers of any type is not known. When they entered the water, the tide flowed out of the bay at 7-9 knots, but no one knew where they intended to go. What is known is that they were working in the tire repair shop at Alcatraz, so they had access to rubber, tools, and other supplies necessary for making a raft or similar flotation device. A guard making rounds saw them at 1 p.m., but when he returned at 1:30 pm., they were gone.[37]

The alarm sounded, and the guards began a massive search for the men. Roe and Cole had cut through two iron bars before smashing a glass window to escape the building. They used a wrench from the tire shop to break a lock on an outside gate. Once through this exit, they were outside the wire fencing surrounding the cellblock and workshops. The guards traced them to the edge of a 20-foot drop, where the trail ended. No further trace of them was ever found at Alcatraz Island or in San Francisco Bay.[38]

Prison authorities naturally proclaimed that no one could have survived swimming across the bay's frigid waters to reach the mainland alive. This did not stop law enforcement from launching a massive search:

> The two were missing at the noon checkup, and officials expressed belief they had escaped over a stockade and climbed down to the shores of the 12-acre

---

[36] *Ibid.*
[37] Tony Pettinato, "Did Two Cons Escape from 'Escape-Proof' Alcatraz?," GenealogyBank (blog), December 16, 2016, accessed November 4, 2024, https://blog.genealogybank.com/did-two-cons-escape-from-escape-proof-alcatraz.html.
[38] *Ibid.*

island where the federal government keeps its worst convicts.

Various officials expressed doubt the pair could reach the mainland without the aid of a boat or raft, but nevertheless a strong police patrol was posted along the San Francisco shore.

So dense was a low-lying fog that Coast Guard and police boats were seriously hampered in searching for the men, one serving 99 years for bank robbery, the other 50 years for kidnapping.

The police launch D.A. White halted its search at dark when visibility was reduced to less than 50 feet, but several Coast Guard craft continued to circle the island and cruise out toward the Golden Gate, where there was a strong ebb tide.[39]

The fog was so thick that it obscured everything more than 50 feet from the boats and the sentries placed to watch along the shoreline. No sightings were made of Cole or Roe in the bay, nor did any of the men spaced along the shore spot them or their bodies. They were never seen again – at least in California. The Associated Press reported that clues of a possible escape were found. Federal agents focused on what appeared to be part of a lifeboat that turned up in the Yacht Harbor, about 1½ miles southeast of Alcatraz Island between Fort Mason and Fort Point at the Presidio. This vicinity is critical in another Alcatraz escape, which will be discussed in the next chapter. The wreckage was not the only possible evidence of escape investigated by authorities. A "mysterious launch" was observed by a "special officer" who called police after he saw it near Richmond on the northeastern shore of the bay. The launch vanished into the fog before authorities could arrive. In the same vicinity, a man pulled a rowboat under an abandoned

---

[39] "Two Flee Alcatraz, 'Escape-Proof Isle, Fog Hinders Search'", various national newspapers, December 17, 1937.

wharf at Richmond and left it there before he, too, vanished before law enforcement could investigate.[40]

By December 20, Warden James Johnston began to think twice about whether Cole and Roe had died in San Francisco Bay. Wire Service reports picked up by Oklahoma Newspapers indicated that Johnston was learning more about the escape and that it had been planned for months. The warden disclosed to the press that the window through which the men escaped was 34 inches tall and 18 inches deep but only 8 inches wide. It was crisscrossed with iron bars and heavy glass, but Roe and Cole had sawed away at the bars for just a few minutes each day over months until they managed to cut through them. He also reported that they likely padded themselves with rubber tire parts before leaping from the 20-foot cliff to the rocky shore below. Once in the water, Johnston believed that the inmates were picked up by a boat as part of "an elaborate plot with everything worked out in detail."[41]

Despite the warden's growing conviction that the escape was planned and successful, federal agents continued to scour the shoreline of San Francisco Bay. They were still searching on December 27, when fog so thick that it duplicated the conditions of the escape day hampered their work.[42]

As far as the citizens of Oklahoma were concerned, Ted Roe and Ralph Cole's survival was unquestioned. They were not surprised when a flurry of reports emerged from various points in California six days after the escape that Cole and Roe had been seen and were headed for Muskogee. Eyewitness sightings of the men came in from Crockett, a town just north of Richmond, where the mysterious launch and rowboat were reported. From there, the sightings followed a trail north into Sonoma County, then in a broad sweep east around San Francisco,

---

[40] "6-Men Search for Cole, Roe After Escape: Agents Refuse to Take It For Grant Alcatraz Convicts Drowned," AP report in *The Ada Evening News*, December 19, 1937.
[41] "Alcatraz Warden Believes Prisoners Escaped Alive In Boat Waiting In Bay," UPI story reprinted in *The Altus Times-Democrat*, December 20, 1937.
[42] "Fog 'Blinds' Frisco", AP story in the *Miami News-Record*, December 27, 1937.

and off to the southwest through Merced County. Agents heard from one witness who knew them that they were going home to Oklahoma.[43]

Sightings of Ralph Roe and Ted Cole followed in Oklahoma, including some connected to minor crimes. No one could ever prove whether they were there or not. The Federal Bureau of Investigation was never as convinced as the Bureau of Prisons that the men drowned in San Francisco Bay. In fact, in 1939, Roe and Cole were named Number 2 and Number 3 on the Ten Most Wanted list.[44]

A bizarre incident brought attention to a Denver hospital in April 1940 when a suspect, who gave his name as Elmer Watson, took poison in a suicide attempt, telling police he did so because he feared being returned to prison. Police in Colorado believed that Watson was using an alias and might be Richard Roe. This suspicion led them to send his fingerprints to FBI analysts in Washington, D.C.[45]

The strange story unfolded as Denver Detectives Sam Finnie and John Wells questioned "Watson" on the evening of April 11, 1940. The man suddenly took a "potion" that proved to be a severe poison, then told the investigators that he did not want to be returned to a prison in Walla Walla, Washington, for parole violation. "Watson" was rushed to Denver General Hospital, where he remained in critical condition 24 hours later. A man and a woman accompanying him were taken into custody as part of the investigation. The woman identified a photograph of Ralph Roe as looking like one that "Watson" carried in his wallet, which he had told her was his brother. She also said that a photo of Cole resembled a man who had recently been with "Watson." The woman further told Detective Finnie that "Watson" admitted to

[43] "Tipster Says Pair Heading For City," *Muskogee Daily Phoenix and Times-Democrat*, December 23, 1937; Theodore Cole and Ralph Roe Escape File, 1937-1938, Federal Bureau of Investigation.
[44] "Oklahoma Felons Put At Nos. 2, 3," AP story appearing in *Ocmulgee Daily Times*, August 12, 1939.
[45] "Suicide Attempt Brings Roe Check," INS report in *The Tulsa Tribune*, April 14, 1940.

breaking parole from Walla Walla but, more significantly, said that he "also broke from Alcatraz."[46]

The excitement died quickly, however, when FBI fingerprint analysts determined that the man was not Ralph Roe. Elmer Watson had spent time on Alcatraz, serving one year there for desertion from the U.S. Army when "The Rock" was still a military prison, but he left at the end of his sentence, not as an escapee.[47]

No one with official status ever saw Theodore "Ted" Cole or Ralph Roe again. They did successfully escape Alcatraz. The only question was whether they made it across San Francisco Bay. The mysterious launch and abandoned rowboat at Richmond on the day of the escape, followed by the string of eyewitness reports forming a pattern to the north, east, and southeast of San Francisco, provides reasonable evidence that they did make it across the water by traveling northeast to shore and then evading pursuit.

No matter what they told investigators and guards, prisoners believed the two Oklahomans made it. The escape became an Alcatraz legend, and others quickly tried to follow in their footsteps with less planning and more violent attempts. The results were deadly for guards and inmates alike. When Morris and the Anglin brothers reached Alcatraz Island, the story of what Cole and Roe had done was still very much part of prison lore. Their disappearance had taken place only 25 years earlier, and there were still inmates around who were there when the two men took to the water. The story likely fascinated the three friends, and they probably gathered as much information as possible about what the Oklahoma men had done. If they hoped to succeed in their escape, they needed to know how those before them had done the impossible.

---

[46] "That Man Roe Has Been Found Again," AP story published in the *Morning Examiner*, April 13, 1940.
[47] "Poison Swallower Is Not Ralph Roe," AP story published in the *Enid Morning News*, April 14, 1940.

Chapter Four

The Escape

EIGHTEEN MONTHS AFTER THE REUNION of Clarence and John Anglin with Frank Lee Morris in Alcatraz, headlines and newsreels stunned the nation with the news that the three men had done the impossible. "The spoon proves mightier than the bars of supposedly escape-proof Alcatraz prison," declared the voice of narrator Ed Herlihy of Universal-International News over ominous music in a newsreel that carried the story through theaters across the United States in June 1962. The opening screen blared the headline in giant type: "FLEE ALCATRAZ: Three Convicts Escape 'Rock'."

News coverage leaves little doubt that many authorities and the media believed the three men likely made it across San Francisco Bay. Another newsreel proclaimed, "The escape triggered the greatest manhunt in San Francisco's history as agents of the FBI, Coast Guardsmen, highway patrol, sheriff's deputies, and local police join in the search." Radio and television stations, newspapers, wire services, freelancers, and even fascinated citizens watching from the hills joined the frenzy. "Three bank robbers serving long terms scratched their way through grills covering an air vent," continued Herlihy's narration, "climbed a drainage pipe, and disappeared from the forbidding rock in San Francisco Bay." While they know more details of how the escape was carried out, to this day, more than sixty years later, federal authorities cannot disprove the following declaration of the newsreel writers: "It appears to be the first successful escape from the maximum-security prison." Whether or not the three men survived the waters of the bay, there is no dispute about one thing. They made it out of Alcatraz. Their escape was successful.

Warden Olin Blackwell and other prison officials blamed the embarrassing situation on deterioration and corrosion caused by exposure to the coastal elements. Salty air and water corroded the prison's concrete, iron, and steel. More than $5,000,000 in repairs were needed to secure it. The Anglin brothers and Frank Morris had exposed a secret that the U.S. Bureau of Prisons did not want out—Alcatraz was no longer escape-proof—if it ever had been.

No official has seen the three men since June 11, 1962. Most authorities believe that they drowned in San Francisco Bay or were swept to their doom when severe currents picked up their homemade raft and carried it into the Pacific Ocean. The penitentiary is now a National Park Service site. It doesn't take long for even casual tourists to understand that Morris and the Anglins were aware of the bay's cold water and tidal currents. All inmates at Alcatraz were told of these things during their orientation. Interviews conducted by FBI agents with dozens of former prisoners after the escape verify this fact. Since they were aware of the tides and water temperature, the inmates undoubtedly considered both when planning the date and time of their attempt.

As many previous writers, including prison officials and federal investigators, have noted, their efforts to carry out the escape were ingenious. They converted things that most people would not think of using into tools. A vacuum cleaner motor was transformed into a power drill. The sharpened stems of spoons were used to dig through eroding concrete walls. The covers of notebooks were carved and painted to serve as duplicates of the ventilation grills at the back of their cells, which the inmates were enlarging as escape tunnels.

The Anglin brothers broke through the backs of their cells first, strongly suggesting that – as some other inmates suggested – Clarence Anglin was the leader of the plan. Although another inmate, Allen West,

38

later told authorities – and subsequently retracted his claim – that he was the brains behind the operation, he failed to complete his tunnel in time to join the escape. This suggests that he likely exaggerated his role. The other inmates had been through the corridor behind the cells many times before the night of the escape. Had West been the "mastermind" of the Alcatraz escape, as he claimed, he would have known long before the night of the departure that something was blocking his attempt to expand his vent into a human-sized tunnel. Instead, it is more likely that he either joined the escape effort late or was not willing to put in the hard work of chipping through the back of his cell, which the other men had spent countless hours doing. He subsequently suggested to FBI agents that he inflated his role in a confession because he feared prison authorities. Either way, West spent the rest of his life in federal penitentiaries.

After they broke through into the utility corridor behind their cells, the Anglin boys helped Frank Morris complete his tunnel so that he could join them there. Together, the three climbed up pipes to the top of the cellblock to examine a ventilation shaft through the roof and determine how it could be removed. The operation was long and slow, but they put time, thought, and work into it. The FBI tested the life preservers fabricated by the inmates and found that they would stay inflated for one to three hours without issue and could be easily reinflated using the nozzle the men had included for that purpose. The engineering of the escapees worked. Since they went to such extremes to prepare for their escape and to adapt items around the prison to assist in their elaborate plan, it is unlikely they have jumped into the bay without first studying its currents and water temperatures.

Warden Blackwell and U.S. Bureau of Prisons officials seemed determined to maintain at least the outward appearance that Alcatraz was escape-proof. FBI agents in San Francisco soon expressed doubts behind the scenes. In a phone call to headquarters in Washington just three days after the disappearance of Morris and the Anglin brothers, Special Agent in Charge of the San Francisco Office Frank L. Price reported that while no evidence had been developed that the trio made their way to the mainland, likewise "there is no information to show that they did not."

SAC Price warned authorities in Washington that "the work which the subjects performed in preparation for the escape is fantastic."[48]

He gave the attention to detail that the Anglins and Morris placed on fabricating a recovered life jacket and raft section as examples:

> ...Examination of the Mae West life preserver jacket which was left behind shows great ingenuity in its preparation. Using raincoats as material, the subjects not only sewed the seams but apparently used hot steam pipes to vulcanize these seams to make them air tight. They used a hollow plastic tube, such as is ordinarily contained in small spray devices in bottles, as a means of inflating the jacket. A heavy paperclip was attached to the tube so it could be closed after the jacket was inflated.
>
> The subjects made two rafts. They took only the larger one with them. The small one left behind showed the same ingenuity in construction as did the life jackets.[49]

More than one year after the escape, FBI agents interviewed an inmate at the U.S. Penitentiary in Atlanta who had been at Alcatraz when the escape took place. He told them about another inmate who worked in the clothing issue room and had provided the escapees with the rubberized raincoats they needed to build their raft, life jackets, and other items:

> He stated that [Redacted Inmate Name #2] formerly of the United States Penitentiary, Alcatraz, worked in the clothing issue room and now claims that he furnished subjects with approximately 350 raincoats, which he took from clothing supplies, and that subjects used the raincoats to build a raft which they used in their escape,

---

[48] C.A. Evans to Mr. Belmont, FBI, "Clarence Anglin," file no. 76-26295. "Memorandum to Mr. Belmont," June 14, 1962, Federal Bureau of Investigation.
[49] *Ibid.*

the building of which raft took some six to eight months. The raft was built so it would hold air and could be pumped up.[50]

The information relayed by the inmate was consistent with that developed by the FBI in its investigation of the escape. It became remarkably more so as he continued to repeat what the second inmate–whose name is redacted in the file released by the Bureau–had told him:

> ...[S]ubjects planned to start their escape from the back of the powerhouse building and carry the raft by hand to the beach and then travel to Angel Island and walk down the beach carrying the raft to a point where they could cross over to Susquelana. . .[Redacted Inmate Name #1] further added he has been told that fragments brought in as part of the raft used by subjects in their escape definitely were not parts of the raft used by the subjects, as it was made of different material.[51]

This is where things get very interesting. The unnamed inmate in Atlanta knew that FBI agents had recovered parts of a raft in San Francisco Bay, a fact kept from the public and out of the record. While FBI reports from the 1960s confirmed the discovery of a paddle, life jackets, and packets containing photographs of Anglin family members, they mention only part of an incomplete second raft left behind. They do not confirm – in fact, they do not even mention – that investigators found part of a raft and human footprints at the beach on Angel Island. This information was not confirmed by federal authorities until Supervising Deputy U.S. Marshal Mike Dyke did so fifty years later. "Some teletypes indicate there was possibly a raft recovered on Angel Island," on June 12, 1962, he told

[50] Report of interview conducted at U.S. Penitentiary – Atlanta, June 26, 1963, File #AT 76-2246, Alcatraz Escape File, Federal Bureau of Investigation.
[51] Ibid.

41

CBS San Francisco in February 2011. He further confirmed that one of the teletypes verified that searchers found "footsteps leading away from the raft."[52]

The Angel Island raft story is critical in investigating the Alcatraz escape. Why do the teletypes verified by Deputy Marshal Dyke not appear in the FBI file on the Alcatraz escape? Were they once included? If so, were they removed? If they were removed, who would do it? And when? The surface implication is that someone did not want the information about the raft and footprints on Angel Island to be made public. There is no doubt that the FBI was aware of them. At least one piece of confirmation comes from the FBI itself. Special Agent in Charge Frank Price sent a teletype message to the Marin County Sheriff's Office, California Highway Patrol, and other area departments. It simply said, "Raft believed used by the escapees located on Angel Island." The teletype is not included in the FBI files released to the public. The inmate in Atlanta, however, learned about the plan by Morris and the Anglins to reach the island, and the agent who interviewed him mentioned "fragments brought in as part of the raft used by the subjects" in such a way that it slipped past censors in the bureau. Some of the fragments proved to be from a fishing net, but others were from raincoats and likely came from the actual raft.[53]

The FBI files lack information about teletypes reporting raft fragments and footprints at Angel Island, which makes this statement from the Bureau even more suspicious: "The plan was to steal clothes and a car once on land. But despite the case's high-profile nature, we never uncovered any thefts like this." This claim on the FBI website is a deliberate lie.[54]

---

[52] "Investigator Says 1962 Alcatraz Escapees Likely Survived," CBS San Franciso, https://www.cbsnews.com/sanfrancisco/news/investigator-says-1962-alcatraz-escapees-likely-survived/, published February 8, 2011, Retrieved September 9, 2024.

[53] Teletype sent by SAC Frank Price, June 12, 1962, quoted by "Anglin Brothers Escape From Alcatraz Prison," cityexperiences, https://dev2.cityexperiences.com/blog/anglin-brothers-escape/, Updated on December 1, 2023, Accessed August 1, 2024.

[54] FBI statement posted at www.fbi.com. Retrieved on August 1, 2024.

A car was stolen in Marin County, California, on the night of the Alcatraz escape:

> An all-points bulletin received by the Eureka area office of the Highway Patrol, Humboldt county sheriff's office and local police from Frank L. Price, agent-in-charge of the FBI's San Francisco regional office states that the stolen car is believed to be the get-away vehicle.
>
> The car is a 1955 Chevrolet sedan, license number KPB 076. Color of the car was not given, but it was reported stolen Tuesday morning.
>
> Price's teletype also stated that the three Alcatraz felons, considered "extremely dangerous", are believed to be making an escape try through Marin County.
>
> Verifax copies of the trio's prison identification photos have been broadcast throughout the western area.[55]

The 1955 Chevrolet was blue. The theft was significant, if for no other reason, because the FBI repeatedly denied that any cars were stolen in the Bay Area. The car was later recovered.

Once again, the Federal Bureau of Investigation positively sent out teletypes providing escape-related information to other agencies that did not make it into the official FBI Alcatraz escape file released to the public. Once again, that fact strongly suggests that the escape was successful and that Frank Morris, Clarence Anglin, and John Anglin were alive and at large. Why was this evidence – and all mention of it – removed from the official file? The only logical conclusion is that the Bureau – or an individual or individuals in it – engaged in a cover-up after realizing that the three escapees slipped through their fingers.

---

[55] "All Law Enforcement Agencies Alerted For Thugs In Stolen Auto," UPI report published in *Humboldt Standard*, June 13, 1962, Page 1.

It is worth noting that conditions on San Francisco Bay were calm when the escapees left Alcatraz Island. The tide had completed its flow into the bay, and the ebb or flow back out of it was about to begin. This outward current increased during the hours following their departure. Based on Allen West's statements to the FBI, he last saw Frank Morris at 9:37 p.m. on June 11, 1962. When he finally got through the vent of his cell, climbed to the top of the cellblock, squeezed through the shaft onto the roof, and made it to the point where they went over the edge and down to the ground, there was no sign of the other three. He believed they likely left the island by 10:30 p.m. or no later than 11:00 p.m.[56]

According to an analysis in 1962 by the U.S. Army Corps of Engineers office in Sausalito, which maintained a working model of the bay, the slack tide was at 10:00 p.m. The closer to that time that the Anglins and Morris got their raft into the water, the easier it would have been for them to paddle to Angel Island. If they had headed straight for the bay when West last saw Morris at 9:42 p.m., they would have been right on target to begin their paddle at 10:00 p.m. Not long after 10, the water started flowing back out of the bay through the Golden Gate into the Pacific. The speed of the current increased rapidly until it reached its peak shortly before midnight.[57]

By keeping to the schedule, the escapees would have made good progress to Angel Island before the ebb tide started to flow back out of the bay. The FBI says today that wind, waves, and frigid waters likely got to the men if they tried to make their way to Angel Island, although kids have now made the swim to prove otherwise, and the men were in a well-constructed rubber boat. Is the Bureau right? Post-escape evidence from just six months later throws a real wrench in the works.

Little Alcatraz is a rock 81 yards off the northwest end of Alcatraz Island. The water of San Francisco Bay covers it during many high tides,

[56] Interview of Allen West, June 15, 1962, from Alcatraz Escape File, Federal Bureau of Investigation.
[57] Statement of U.S. Engineer's Office, Sausalito, California, June 12, 1962, from Alcatraz Escape File, Federal Bureau of Investigation.

a fact that has made it a hazard to navigation for centuries. The steamer *Paul Pry* struck it on December 22, 1862, giving it the name Paul Pry Rock, which it held for many years. The British ship *Oliver Cutts* struck it and sank on January 14, 1868. Even today, small pleasure craft run into it on occasion.[58]

Little Alcatraz and Fort Point, located under one end of the Golden Gate Bridge, provide critical evidence supporting the theory that the Anglins and Morris successfully escaped Alcatraz. That's because of what John Paul Scott and Darl Lee Parker did on the evening of Sunday, December 16, 1962, just six months after the Anglin brothers and Frank Lee Morris incident. It was at 5:17 p.m. that guards conducting a routine check discovered that the two men serving time at Alcatraz for bank robbery, escape, and other crimes were missing. The alarm immediately sounded, and a massive search was launched of the prison and its grounds. The prison launch began circling the island and was quickly joined by four Coast Guard cutters. It was not long before Darl Parker was found clinging to Little Alcatraz. He was rescued from the jagged rock and carried back to the prison from which he had escaped. He made it off the island, but his poor swimming abilities left him confounded. Scott, however, could not be found. The boats expanded their search pattern but still found no trace of the missing inmate.

It was not until 8 p.m., some three and one-half hours after the escape, that John Paul Scott finally appeared. His location stunned searchers, prison officials, and inmates alike. A group of teenagers hanging out near Fort Point, beneath the southern end of the Golden Gate Bridge, spotted him sitting on the rocks, resting, at around 8:15 p.m. Not only did Scott escape Alcatraz, but he did so without the raft, life jackets, or any other safety measures employed by John Anglin, Clarence Anglin, or Frank Morris. And he crossed right over the channel that authorities claimed had swept the three men to their deaths in the Pacific.

---

[58] Quintana, Sergio, "Alcatraz Ferry Rescues 10 Passengers from Sinking Boat in SF Bay," NBC Bay Area, published August 4, 2017, Updated August 5, 2017, Retrieved September 14, 2024.

Military Police and an ambulance crew from the Presidio rushed to the scene. Sergeant First Class Morton Field of the ambulance team reported that Scott's only flotation device was a shirt tied around his waist, into which "several pairs of inflated surgical gloves" were inserted to add buoyancy. Using this contraption as a makeshift life belt, he swam two and a half miles from Alcatraz to Fort Point across the main shipping channel. He safely reached shore and was found "sitting on a rock a few feet above the water."[59]

Scott's escape occurred in December, when the San Francisco Bay area was approaching its coldest temperatures. It consisted of swimming two and a half miles with just some inflated surgical gloves stuffed into the sleeves of a shirt for buoyancy. Suddenly, the idea of Frank Morris and the Anglin brothers paddling a rubber raft one mile to Angel Island while wearing life jackets did not seem so preposterous. As for his condition, John Paul Scott spent three hours in colder water than the Anglins and Morris had entered, but according to Col. John Roberts, he quickly recovered from the effects of his swim and was soon smiling and "back to normal."[60]

Only Scott could say whether the three-hour swim and a few minutes of freedom at Fort Point were worth it. He spent the next thirty-four years in federal prison, finally dying in 1986 at the U.S. Penitentiary in Tallahassee, Florida. Although he lived a life of crime and died in prison, he proved by swimming across San Francisco Bay in December 1962 – six months after the much better-known Alcatraz escape - that Frank Morris and the Anglin brothers more likely than not made it to shore and that prison officials were wildly overstating the "impossibility" of the feat. The FBI became significantly more serious about investigating sightings and other tips regarding Clarence, John, and Frank. Too much time and too much information, however, had slipped through their fingers.

---

[59] *Boston Record American*, December 17, 1962; *Omaha World Herald*, December 18, 1962.
[60] Omaha World Herald, December 18, 1962.

Generations of athletes have duplicated John Paul Scott's feat – and then some – since 1962. Participating in an event called the "Escape from Alcatraz" Duathlon, hearty souls not only swim 1.5 miles across San Francisco Bay using wet suits instead of surgical gloves, but they then complete a round-trip run of more than 7 miles along the southern shore of the bay to Fort Point and back from their landing point. Hundreds of people have participated in the event over the decades, proving that the Scott route out of Alcatraz was feasible and that individuals in good physical condition can even complete a long run after the incredible swim. The event also proves that the prison's warnings to inmates about sharks were nothing more than urban legends created to enhance the psychological fear associated with "the Rock." A shark has not attacked anyone during any of the cross-bay swimming events.

Strangely, despite Scott's crossing of the bay just six months later and the events in which thousands of people have swum it from the prison to the mainland or Angel Island since, the FBI maintains to this day that Morris and the Anglins likely drowned. This is the bureau's current statement on their escape:

The Mystery Continues

What happened next remains a mystery. Did they make it across the Bay, get to Angel Island, and then cross Raccoon Strait into Marin County as planned? Or did the wind and waves get the better of them?

Many people have gone to great lengths to prove that the men could have survived, but the question remains: did they indeed survive? Our investigation at the time concluded otherwise for the following reasons:

Crossing the Bay. Yes, youngsters have made the more than mile-long swim from Alcatraz to Angel Island. But with the strong currents and frigid Bay water, the odds were clearly against these men.

47

Three if by land. According to our prison informant, the plan was to steal clothes and a car once on land. However, despite the high-profile nature of the case, we never uncovered any thefts of this nature.

Family ties. If the escapees had help, we couldn't substantiate it. The families appeared unlikely to even have the financial means to provide any real support.

Missing in action. For the 17 years we worked on the case, no credible evidence emerged to suggest the men were still alive, either in the U.S. or overseas.[61]

---

[61] FBI statement posted at www.fbi.com. Retrieved on August 1, 2024.

Chapter Five

A Story from the Houston County Jail

MANY STORIES HAVE EMERGED about the Alcatraz escapees since they fled the prison on June 11, 1962, but the most bizarre by far was told by an inmate at the Houston County Jail in Alabama. This jail was quite familiar to the Anglin Brothers; it was where they spent time while on trial for robbing the Bank of Columbia. The story is so strange that it makes you think twice, even today.

It began when Houston County Sheriff James Herring contacted the FBI office in Mobile. A prisoner enjoying the hospitality of his jail wanted to talk to an FBI agent. He claimed to have information on the whereabouts of Frank Morris, John Anglin, and Clarence Anglin. The sheriff warned that he thought the individual was "some sort of a 'psycho'." [62]

Nevertheless, the Special Agent in Charge in Mobile sent a Special Agent to Dothan to interview the prisoner. The sheriff was correct; the inmate had a strange story to tell:

> In June 1962, he received a telephone call from an
> unnamed individual. As he was not at the residence, the

---

[62] Special Agent in Charge, Mobile, Alabama to Special Agent in Charge, Atlanta, Georgia, September 4, 1962. FBI, "Clarence Anglin," file no. 76-26295.

caller did not leave a message with his mother. Subsequently the same day [long redaction by the FBI including identity and other information about the caller] and further, whom he had known at the Federal Penitentiary, Atlanta, who advised [the prisoner] if [the prisoner] could obtain a suitable legitimate residence to be used as a hideout then [the prisoner] could pick up about $5,000. [The caller] stated that some people, number not stated, needed the hideout and [the caller] was too hot to provide same, so he was requesting [the prisoner's] assistance. [The prisoner said] he would see what he could do and to contact him later.[63]

The FBI blacked out the caller's identity and all information about him when the document was released to the public. From the info left accessible, he identified himself as a former acquaintance of the Houston County Jail inmate from the U.S. Penitentiary in Atlanta. The subsequent investigation confirmed that the informant had been formerly incarcerated at the Atlanta penitentiary. Since he had informed the sheriff in Dothan that he had information to provide about the Alcatraz escapees, it is also apparent that the hideout was for them. Some time passed, but sure enough, the intermediary called again:

> …About a week or ten days later, which would be around 7/5/62 [the caller] and subject FRANK LEE MORRIS came to [long section of report redacted here by the FBI, but ends with indication that they came to the prisoner's home in a black 1959 Lincoln]. [The prisoner] stated positively it was FRANK LEE MORRIS, and identified a photograph of MORRIS as the person who accompanied [the caller] to the residence as stated above.[64]

---

[63] *Ibid.*
[64] *Ibid.*

On the surface, this tale sounds unbelievable. Nevertheless, a check of records at the U.S. Penitentiary in Atlanta revealed that not only had the inmate in Dothan served time there, but he also played on the prison baseball team with Frank Lee Morris, whom he knew well. One of the seldom-mentioned facts about Morris is that he was a better-than-average baseball player. The athletic abilities of the Anglin brothers, who grew up outdoors and spent much of their time working as farm laborers, are often mentioned in stories about their escape. Morris – the smallest in stature of the three – is usually treated as the "city boy." He was an avid athlete who loved baseball, closely followed the sport, and often listened to the games on the radio. Those who knew him at various prisons over the years remembered that he was always among the best players. That the inmate sitting in jail in Dothan played on the team with Morris suggests that he knew Frank well and that, whatever his mental state, he was likely a skilled baseball player as well.[65]

The inmate told FBI agents that Morris and the intermediary took him from his home in College Park, Georgia – a suburb of Atlanta – to Langley, South Carolina. Langley is across the Savannah River from Georgia and about 35 miles northeast of Augusta via today's SC-425. When the trio arrived in Langley, they went to a cabin he thought was "possibly called Langley Pond." After some discussions that he did not describe, he left, telling the men to stay until he could get in touch:

> …About a week later, around 7/12/62 [the inmate] went to this cabin, where he saw [the intermediary], MORRIS, subject JOHN ANGLIN and another individual, whose face he did not see, but whom he presumed was subject CLARENCE ANGLIN, and he also saw the same black 1959 Lincoln. After a short conversation MORRIS gave [the inmate] $150 to rent a place in the country, with the

---

[65] FBI, "Clarence Anglin," file no. 76-26295.

instructions that [he, the inmate] should contact MORRIS
later for the rest of the $5,000.[66]

The inmate told agents that "he became afraid of this group, so he
decided to keep the $150" and head for Alabama instead. He called another
associate who knew the intermediary, told him he was "going to Alabama
to look for a hideout," and would subsequently notify him to give the
intermediary its location. He went straight to Houston County, where he
found a place. There is no indication in the FBI file that he had ever been
in the area before. He was soon picked up driving a stolen car and found
himself in the Houston County Jail. Suffering from a hurt back, he was
sent to the Cobb Memorial Hospital in Phenix City for treatment. While
there, he contacted his friend and asked him to notify the intermediary with
news that "he had found a place in Alabama." He also asked for help as he
"needed someone to get him out on bond."[67]

He spent a little over ten days at the hospital in Phenix City for
treatment of his injuries, during which time, according to his claims, two
men showed up for a shocking visit:

> ...[The inmate] stated around 1:00 or 2:00 a.m., Monday,
> 8/20/62 subject MORRIS and [the intermediary] came to
> visit him briefly at Cobb Memorial Hospital and advised
> they would send a bondsman to get him out of jail. He has
> not heard from them since that time. [The inmate] stated
> another patient was in the same room at the hospital who
> possibly would be able to verify his story.[68]

The inmate openly confirmed that he had spent 30 days in a South
Carolina mental health facility earlier in his life. He also told FBI agents
that he participated in group therapy sessions for three years while

---

[66] SAC Mobile to SAC Atlanta, September 4, 1962
[67] *Ibid.*
[68] *Ibid.*

incarcerated in the U.S. Penitentiary – Atlanta. The nature of his illness was not disclosed in the FBI files.[69]

As the sheriff had warned, it was a bizarre story. How much, if any, of it could be true? First, it must be distinctly understood that it is not uncommon for inmates to exaggerate events and their importance in them to secure favors or preferred treatment for themselves. This is especially true with recidivists who have a history of being in and out of jail and prison, which was the situation with the inmate in this case. It was common in FBI interviews with other inmates about the Alcatraz escape. Allen West, the fourth inmate involved in the escape attempt, is a good example. He initially expanded his role in the escape but later revised his statement and reduced his claims. West blamed his initial statements on fear of guards at Alcatraz, but he seemed caught up in the moment. The point is that while the inmate in the Houston County Jail undoubtedly exaggerated and made some fictional claims in his statement, this does not mean that he did not include a thread of truth. If there was any truth in what he said, what could it have been?

The FBI Field Office in San Francisco insisted that agents in the Southeast investigate the matter thoroughly. Skeptical agents from Atlanta interviewed the inmate's parents at their home in College Park on September 6, 1962. Aside from a note that the parents admitted their son "is possibly sick mentally and cannot be trusted and is a known liar," the FBI redacted virtually the entire report before releasing it to the public. Eight of nine paragraphs either have long redactions or were wholly redacted. The only other information left intact was that his parents, unsurprisingly, insisted that Frank Lee Morris had not been in their home and that they last remembered an ex-con visiting their son the previous April or May.[70]

---

[69] *Ibid.*
[70] SAC San Francisco Field Office to Director FBI, September 13, 1962, FBI, "Clarence Anglin," file no. 76-26295.; SAC Atlanta to SAC San Francisco, September 10, 1962, FBI, "Clarence Anglin," file no. 76-26295.

The Atlanta Special Agent in Charge's report was followed by instructions for other FBI offices, which provide some clues to what was included in its redacted paragraphs. The Mobile office, for example, was instructed to re-interview the inmate in Dothan to identify the ex-con who visited him at his parent's home in April or May and to ascertain "the name of the individual who came in a late model dark car" and find out "who is the person who allegedly drove him from Columbia to Fairview, S.C." The agents were to find out "if this is the same individual who drove a 1959 Mercury." This is curious because any discussion is redacted from the report itself. Still, the instructions appear to indicate that the inmate's parents confirmed that he had been in South Carolina as he told FBI agents, that he somehow got from his home to Columbia – which would have taken him right past Langley – and that someone drove him from Columbia to Fairview in a "late model dark car." It was not the late model Blue Chevrolet stolen in Marin County, California, on the night of the Alcatraz escape.[71]

Why would the FBI redact this information from a report more than 60 years after the fact, but leave in detail about the mental health of the inmate who triggered this phase of the investigation? Possibly because the agency covered up teletypes about raft parts being found at Angel Island and lied about car theft in Marin County on the night of the escape?

There was more. The Savannah office was also put on the hunt for the individual who drove the Dothan inmate from Columbia to Fairview Crossroads near Wagner, South Carolina. Fairview Crossroads is about halfway between Langley and Columbia. Agents were also to investigate the cabin at Langley to "develop information concerning subjects' whereabouts." The Atlanta SAC signaled other agents his opinion about San Francisco's request when he wrote, "Even though [Dothan inmate's] own mother admits he is a mental case, it is felt that San Francisco, as the origin, desires this possible lead checkout to locate subjects."[72]

---

[71] *Ibid.*
[72] *Ibid.*

Agents from the Mobile office interviewed the inmate at the Houston County Jail in Dothan a second time on September 14, 1962. There were no changes in his story:

> ...He continued to affirm that the information he had previously furnished was substantially correct. He claims to have seen MORRIS at [his parents'] residence as previously related. He stated that the ex-convict who had visited him at [his parents'] residence in the early summer of 1962 was [redacted], whose last name he could not recall, whom he had met at the Federal Penitentiary.[73]

Once again, the FBI redacted long portions of the report on the inmate's interview before releasing it to the public. Reading between the redactions, he appears to have told the agents from Mobile that his parents had no connection with the information he had furnished about Morris and the Anglin brothers.

Agents from Savannah tried to follow the directions that the inmate gave in his first interview and locate the cabin by the lake or pond where he said Morris and the Anglin brothers were hiding when he saw them:

> In reference to [Dothan inmate's] directions to a cabin on the lake near Warrenville, South Carolina, it is to be noted that U.S. Highway 1 includes U.S. Highway 78, which is a four-lane highway approximately 15 years old between Augusta and Aiken, which bypasses Langley, South Carolina and Warrenville, South Carolina, as described by [the inmate]. The highway is now known as the Aiken-Augusta Road and in following this road as directed. . . one goes to Langley, South Carolina, to the Post office and turning left on a dirt road and crossing a

---

[73] San Francisco Field Office Report, October 10, 1962, pp. 80-82, FBI, "Clarence Anglin," file no. 76-26295.

bridge which is a dam over Horse Creek, which holds Horse Creek Lake, also known as Langley Pond. His directions of turning right immediately after the bridge on a dirt road takes one on a dirt road with a large gate, leading to the United Merchants Clubhouse. There are no lakes or cabins other than this clubhouse on this side of the lake. There is no road making a sharp left turn off this road at this distance, especially one and one-half miles to two miles which would, if existed, cross the four-lane highway to either Jordantown, Sunset Memorial Gardens Cemetery, or the Midland Country Club, which is north of the dual-lane highway. A physical check of both sides of Langley Pond and inquiries among life-long residents failed to develop any information concerning a cabin in the area on a dead-end road.[74]

The landscape around Langley, South Carolina, has undergone significant changes since 1962, but the key features described by the inmate remain. When you turn left from the central intersection, you immediately pass the dam over Horse Creek, which forms Langley Pond. He told FBI agents that he "thought" the lake he saw might have been named Langley Pond, but what if he wasn't describing the lake immediately in town? What if it were a different lake on the same road but a little deeper in the woods? Just after passing Langley Pond, the road described by the inmate crosses under U.S. 1/U.S. 78 and becomes Sudlow Pond Road. If you continue to follow it, at 2 ½ miles out, you will come to Sudlow Pond. Suppose you apply the inmate's directions to historical maps illustrating the area of this pond. In that case, you achieve entirely different results than the FBI agents did when they tried it with Langley Pond. After crossing the bridge over Little Horse Creek at the foot of the pond, there was a dirt road to the right, as he described. From this point, it was possible to follow this road until you reached a sharp left, precisely at

---

[74] *Ibid.*

the distance he described. If you followed this road as described, you would go to a spot where you could park and walk to a cabin on the lake, once again exactly as the inmate had described.[75]

What can be made of the story from the Houston County Jail? Some of it is undoubtedly fanciful. For example, Frank Morris visiting the hospital in Phenix City is a stretch. On the other hand, why would an ex-con with no known connection to the Wiregrass region suddenly leave his parents' home in Atlanta to find a safe place to live in Houston County, Alabama? He was unemployed and depended on his parents for support. Where did he get the money to go unless, as he said, someone gave him $150?

Likewise, FBI agents confirmed – despite the efforts of censors at the Bureau to redact the information – that the inmate had traveled extensively in South Carolina just as he said and at the time that he said. They even tracked down the intermediary that he named. By September, he was in Georgia's Fulton County Jail, where he had been confined after an August arrest. He admitted that he knew the informant and expressed animosity against him, calling him a "punk." He denied being involved with the escapees and denied seeking the inmate's help. Nevertheless, his whereabouts in June and July 1962 were not accounted for.[76]

The inmate's claim that Frank Morris gave him $150 but promised $5,000 more once he completed his assignment is interesting. It fits a pattern established in allegations that the inmates and their associates bribed guards at Alcatraz to look the other way as they were working on their escape plan. A serious investigation of these allegations took place after the escape, with guards refusing to speak to FBI agents and inmates telling investigators that they had assisted in arranging payment deliveries to prison employees. The pattern was exactly as described by the inmate in the Houston County Jail. Guards were allegedly given smaller amounts

---

[75] Recreation of route described by inmate using 2024 Google Maps and historical maps from the Perry-Castenada Library Map Collection, University of Texas Libraries, The University of Texas at Austin.
[76] FBI, "Clarence Anglin," file no. 76-26295.

upfront but rewarded with large quantities later. Frank Morris, who had the most significant prison account, was the name most often associated with these bribes. He also had associates in New Orleans who were willing to help.[77]

The Dothan inmate knew Frank Morris from prison in Atlanta. He may have also known John and Clarence Anglin, but he and Frank played baseball together. When the FBI sought out known acquaintances and family members of Morris and the Anglin brothers after the escape to see if they had heard from them, this individual was not on their list. He was precisely the type of "off the radar" friend that Morris might have contacted through an intermediary if he needed help.

The FBI failed to find the cabin near what may have been Langley Pond while trying to follow the inmate's directions. However, just 2 ½ miles away on the same road was a second pond with dirt roads and a cabin that matched his description almost precisely. Whether Frank Morris, John Anglin, and Clarence Anglin were ever in that cabin is impossible to know, because FBI agents did not take the tip seriously enough to consider that their informant might be referring to the next pond down the road.

Finally, it is worth noting that the inmate tried to find a hideout for the escapees on turf familiar to them in the Wiregrass area. He had no intimate knowledge of Houston County and the surrounding area, but they did. There is no indication in the FBI files that agents even considered that the Alcatraz three were planning a return to the vicinity.

---

[77] FBI, "Clarence Anglin," file no. 76-26295.

Chapter Six

Bank Robbery in Jay, Florida

SOMETHING UNEXPECTED HAPPENED as FBI agents were interviewing an inmate at the U.S. Penitentiary in Atlanta, Georgia. The prisoner was very nervous about talking to agents, explaining that he would be a "dead man" if it got out that he was furnishing information to the Bureau. He specifically requested "that his identity under no circumstances be made known to any outside individual during the conducting of [this] investigation." The demand was underlined in the FBI's description of the interview, one of the few instances where this occurs in the thousands of pages of federal documents about the Alcatraz escape.[78]

The prisoner of interest to FBI agents knew all three Anglin brothers, having "built time" with one or more of them at Florida State Prison in Raiford or Georgia State Prison in Reidsville. Upon his arrival in Atlanta, he found Alfred Anglin serving time at the penitentiary and the two resumed their friendship. Around April 1962, Alfred told him Clarence and John were planning an escape from Alcatraz. It is a fact that other inmates on "The Rock" knew about the planned escape before it took place, but it is fascinating to consider that the news could have traveled

---

[78] Inmate Interview at U.S. Penitentiary – Atlanta, February 28, 1964, FBI, "Clarence Anglin," file no. 76-26295.

across the country to the federal prison in Atlanta before the fact. Subsequent reports indicate that guards in California were disciplined over allegations of accepting bribes for passing messages and other infractions, rendering such cross-country communication possible.

The inmate himself did not believe that anyone could escape Alcatraz and "did not place much stock in this prediction until it happened about two months later." He was as surprised as anyone else when Frank Morris, John Anglin, and Clarence Anglin disappeared. He told agents that Alfred Anglin initially had no other source for information about them than the media:

> Following the escape, when the newspapers were reporting the Subjects were presumed dead, ANGLIN was very morose and gloomy, but shortly thereafter, he received a visit from another brother, known as [Robert Anglin, Jr.] and from that point on ANGLIN was his normal, cheery self again.
>
> Subsequent to this, Anglin commented to him on several occasions that the Subjects were alive and well, and in fact he was certain they had "hit the bank of Jay," Jay Florida, which was "hit" about one year ago. He stated ANGLIN never mentioned where the subjects could be located....[79]

Jay is a small town just south of the Alabama border, about 43 miles north of Pensacola, Florida. On today's highways, it is a 2 ½ to 3-hour drive west of Dothan. The Bank of Jay was only 11 years old in January 1963. The giant Jay Oil and Gas Field was still seven years away from discovery, but the bank had significant cash on hand and a steady stream of deposits coming in daily. In many ways, it was like the Bank of Columbia, which had been targeted by the Anglin brothers just five years earlier. Both were in secondary towns located near a state border. Both had significant cash deposits. Both locations offered quick access to large rural areas, eliminating the possibility of traffic or other

---

[79] *Ibid.*

obstructions that might hinder a quick getaway. Neither bank had a guard. Neither bank had ever been successfully robbed. Similarities to the Bank of Columbia robbery become even more apparent when the Jay crime is examined.

The Jay robbery occurred as one of the coldest weather systems in years barreled down on Northwest Florida. The *Pensacola News Journal* reported that Wednesday, January 23, 1963—the day of the robbery— recorded a high temperature of 68 degrees at 2:30 p.m. Just 90 minutes later, the thermometer read 38 degrees. It was 20 degrees at midnight and fell to 16-18 by the following day. With what the newspaper described as this "Dr. Jekyll and Mr. Hyde weather" on the way, the employees of the Bank of Jay were already having a stressful day. Six bank examiners were there.[80]

Their day got much more stressful at noon when two well-dressed men in gray plastic raincoats walked in. They wore dark trousers and shined shoes, were not wearing masks, and each carried a snub-nosed, nickel-plated revolver. One was said to be 6 feet tall, 190 pounds, with a slender build, fair complexion, and "lots of light brown hair" [FBI reports of the robbery say "blonde"]. The other was 5'8" tall, 160 pounds, medium build, dark wavy hair, and a broad forehead. Each was clean-shaven. Bank employees estimated that the taller robber was around 30 years old, while they believed the shorter one was around 27 years old. Bank President Price W. Malone told reporters that the robbers seemed surprised by how many people were present when they walked in. "They had cased the bank before."[81]

John Anglin had blonde hair that probably appeared a bit darker when styled with the hair products preferred by men in the 1950s and

---

[80] "Pensacola Slammed By Cold," *Pensacola News Journal*, January 24, 1963; Jim Watley, "$54,611 Loss Fixed In Jay Bank Holdup," *Pensacola News Journal*, January 24, 1963.
[81] Jim Watley, "$54,611 Loss Fixed in Jay Bank Holdup," *Pensacola News Journal*, January 24, 1963; John Hodgkins, "Bandits Meant Business, Says Jay Bank Head," *Pensacola News Journal*, January 24, 1963; FBI, "Clarence Anglin," file no. 76-26295.

early 1960s. Since he preferred to sweep it high on his head, it also made him appear slightly taller than his 5'10". Frank Morris had a "broad" forehead, "dark wavy hair," and was 5'7½" tall. He was older than 27 years, as estimated by the bank employees, but he looked young. J. Earle Bowden, the legendary editor of the *Pensacola News Journal*, drew sketches of the two robbers. One bears a striking likeness to Frank Lee Morris, especially in the forehead and hair.[82]

The robbers cleared the tellers' cash drawers and forced a bank employee to open the safe. They got away with $54,611. The bank employees, examiners, and several customers – including an 8-year-old boy – were forced to remain on the floor and told not to move for 5 minutes. They ignored this warning and called the police when the outlaws left the bank and fled.

To this day, the Bank of Jay robbery has not been solved. Speculation focused on men from Pensacola, one of whom was a decorated police officer. However, speculation and proof are two different things. Speculation has ruined the reputation of many innocent people. A quick focus on suspects without evidence can also lead to crimes not being solved. Be that as it may, speculation on local individuals continues to be a defining element of the Bank of Jay robbery. The FBI raised eyebrows internally about this in the 1960s, especially after the inmate in Atlanta relayed the information that Alfred Anglin had given him:

[Redacted much of sentence] Bank of Jay said there is a resemblance between JOHN ANGLIN and FRANK MORRIS with the unknown subjects but they are not the subjects.

[President Price W. Malone] Bank of Jay, advised that though there is a resemblance between JOHN ANGLIN and FRANK MORRIS and the robbers of the bank, he is sure that [two suspects from Pensacola] robbed the bank. Shortly after the robbery some newspaper in Alabama speculated that the

---

[82] *Pensacola News Journal*, February 24, 1963.

ANGLINS and MORRIS had robbed the Bank of Jay and had printed their photographs along with the article. This article received quite a bit of comment at that time.[83]

With local investigators determined to pin the robbery on individuals in the area and having convinced bank executives and employees of the guilt of these suspects, there was little the FBI could do. Whether or not Morris and the Anglins carried out the crime, the similarities between it and the Bank of Columbia robbery warrant attention. In addition to the robbers' actions inside the bank, it was evident to the bank president that the men had staked out the institution before attempting the heist to select a time when few people would be present. The Anglin brothers employed this same plan at Columbia in 1958. Some of the language used by the robbers was the same. The use of two cars was another hallmark that is very similar to the crime in Columbia. The men drove north from Pensacola in two vehicles before the robbery, leaving one at the elementary school's parking lot in Century, Florida, while they drove the other to Jay for the theft. This was not unlike the Anglin brothers, who left one car in Bainbridge while they drove the other to Columbia for the holdup there. After completing the crime, they fled west back to Century at high speed, outrunning efforts to put up roadblocks. The car used to travel to and from Jay was a 1961 blue-green Ford Falcon Futura. Billed as the "compact cousin of the Thunderbird," it was small and fast. The car was also hot. It had been stolen from Auto Center on West Garden Street in Pensacola on January 13.[84]

The robbers abandoned the Falcon Futura at nearby Century Elementary School and fled together in a white or cream-colored 1959 Chevrolet. Where they went from there was anyone's guess, but by the next day, they were back in Pensacola. A sales clerk at Hess Marine on New Warrington Road later remembered haggling with them over the

---

[83] Report from Jay, included in Report of Special Agent, San Francisco Field Office, June 26, 1964, FBI, "Clarence Anglin," file no. 76-26295.

[84] *Pensacola News Journal* coverage January 14, 1963 – February 24, 1963.

price of an aluminum Coleman cooler. Receipt duplicates showed that it was purchased on January 14, 1963, the day after the bank robbery in Jay. In probably the most bizarre occurrence, the same cooler was found by a "ragpicker" east of Ninth Avenue between Creighton and Olive Roads in Pensacola on February 10, 1963.[85]

Rag picking is a profession that has gone the way of the Ford Falcon Futura. The name survives to a degree in the "pickers" of the 21st century. They struggled to survive by going through others' trash and garbage, looking for rags to sell in bulk to paper manufacturers. They also sought any other items that might have value. In this case, he discovered a recently disturbed spot while scouring a wooded area, looking for metal scraps to sell. He dug up the recently covered hole and found the metal Coleman cooler. When he opened it, the poor but honest man was stunned to discover it contained $40,220.[86]

FBI Special Agent-in-Charge D.K. Brown, Jr., of the Jacksonville Field Office, told local reporters that, according to lab analysis, the cooler had been dug up once before, but he could not explain why. Perhaps it was to remove some of the loot since slightly over $10,000 was missing? Thanks to the unidentified finder's honesty, the FBI recovered the rest of the money and even attempted a stakeout of the site to see if those who buried the cooler would return. No one ever did. SAC Brown praised the man who found the money, describing him as an individual of "very modest means" but possessed with "extreme honesty." It is worth noting that Hoover Insurance Company of New York never gave him so much as one penny as a reward for recovering over $40,000 that it stood to lose due to the robbery. Their policy, they stated, was not to hand out rewards.[87]

---

[85] *Ibid.*

[86] William Prime, "Scavenging Ragpicker Finds Jay Bank Loot," *Pensacola News Journal*, February 24, 1963.

[87] *Ibid.*; Continuing *Pensacola News Journal* coverage, February 25, 1963 – March 25, 1964.

The behind-the-scenes attempt to blame the robbery on a Pensacola police officer blew up on November 27, 1963. The headline "Ingram Loses; Bank Robbery Probe Is Told" appeared above the fold in the *Pensacola Journal* that day. According to the article by reporter Paul Jasper, the City Civil Service Board found against Officer L.J. Ingram the previous day by a vote of 2-1 on a charge of insubordination. The vote came because the officer refused to dress up like a robber on the orders of Pensacola Police Chief D.P. Caldwell after Bank of Jay President Price W. Malone and Vice President Jesse Golden failed to identify him as either of the robbers during an initial lineup:

> About an hour later, he returned and was handed a raincoat and dark glasses—similar to that worn by one of the Jay bandits—and told to don them for further inspection of the two men.
>
> Ingram objected. He was then given a direct order by Caldwell to do so.
>
> Ingram then asked if he could confer with his attorneys. He was given an hour to do so.
>
> Upon his return, Ingram again refused to don the raincoat and glasses.
>
> Caldwell suspended him later that same day on charges of insubordination and failure to obey an order. (The board subsequently dropped that charge.)[88]

Attempting to force Ingram to participate in a second lineup one hour after the first, limiting the time that he could consult his attorney, charging him with insubordination for refusing to dress like one of the robbers, and more about this situation raise serious questions about violations of the officer's rights under the U.S. Constitution. Additional questions of a possible attempted setup arose when the reporter revealed

---

[88] Paul Jasper, "Ingram Loses; Bank Robbery Probe Is Told," *Pensacola Journal*, November 27, 1963.

that the two bank officials were shown a photograph of Ingram before the lineup and, even then, still could not positively identify him as one of the two robbers. It was at this point, according to the officer's testimony, that his supervisors tried to dress him up like the bank robber:

> When he arrived back at the chief's office, he said, he was met by Inspector E.A. Lawhon and handed the raincoat and glasses. He said he inquired the reason.
>
> "Well, you are supposed to be the robber," he quoted Lawhon as saying. "This is what he wore and this is what we want you to wear."
>
> At that point Ingram requested the conference with the chief, and then subsequently consulted his attorneys, Forsyth Carol and his partner, Joe Harrell. Both lawyers, he said, advised him that such a lineup was "unfair" and "dangerous" because he might be mistakenly identified.[89]

Chief Caldwell responded to Officer Ingram's statements by saying that the two bank officers had "tentatively identified" him as the robber during the first lineup. Golden had said that Ingram "looked very much like the man near the holdup but he couldn't definitely identify him." Malone, the bank president, on the other hand, "would be willing to testify Ingram was the man that held a gun on him." The chief further admitted that "the bank officials earlier had seen a picture of Ingram." Showing witnesses a photo of a suspect before having that suspect appear in a lineup is highly questionable.[90]

Testimony also revealed that Ingram had cooperated in the investigation shortly after the Jay robbery due to his resemblance to one of the robbers. He went with investigators to the location where the Coleman cooler used to hide the money was purchased to see if employees could identify him as the man they negotiated with – they

[89] *Ibid.*
[90] *Ibid.*

could not. He even offered to go with FBI agents to see eyewitnesses at the bank, but agents did not feel this was necessary. After the questionable lineup fiasco, he had asked the FBI to leave him alone.[91]

Sergeant Oscar Henderson of the Pensacola Police Department testified about the officer's good character and long history of outstanding and honest work. Former Sheriff Henry Clay Mitchell of Santa Rosa County testified that he disapproved of the attempt to force Ingram to dress up like one of the robbers.[92]

Deep in the article, the writer noted that in addition to L.J. Ingram, a second Pensacola police officer was also suspected in the Jay robbery and that testimony in the hearing mentioned that fact. His name was never mentioned, but discussion was made of a second lineup held on the same day as the Ingram one. Bank executives must have failed even tentatively to identify the second officer in connection with the robbery. Mention was also made that Ingram had offered to travel to Marianna since the FBI had questioned him about a bank robbery there due to his resemblance to one of the suspects. That robbery will be discussed in the next chapter.[93]

Officer L.J. Ingram of the Pensacola Police Department was unfortunate in that he resembled not only the man who robbed the Bank of Jay in January 1963 but Frank Lee Morris, too. Or could the bank robber and Morris have been the same man? So much attention was placed on Ingram as a suspect in the months after the robbery that whoever did the robbery disappeared into the fabric of time. Eighty percent of the money from the crime was recovered. Officer Ingram served his 30-day suspension and then returned to his job with the department, where he continued to enforce the law in Pensacola for years to come.

---

[91] *Ibid.*

Chapter Seven

Citizens State Bank Robbery in Marianna, Florida

Marianna is the county seat of Jackson County. Seminole County, Georgia, is just over the Chattahoochee River to the east, and Houston County, Alabama, is across the state line to the north. The Bank of Columbia, robbed by the Anglin brothers in 1958, is 42 miles northeast of Marianna. The Bank of Jay, where robbers matching the descriptions of John Anglin and Frank Morris struck in January 1963, is 125 miles northwest. Blountstown, where Alfred Anglin caught a bus to pick up the second getaway car after the Columbia robbery, is 28 miles southeast. Jackson County was connected to the places the Anglins lived and knew as kids, and they passed through while fleeing pursuit in 1958 on their way to Blountstown. Clarence knew the name Marianna exceptionally well. He spent thirteen months there at the Florida Industrial School for Boys (later called the Arthur G. Dozier School for Boys).[94]

Arrested in Hillsborough County on June 2, 1945, for breaking & entering and larceny, the 14-year-old future bank robber was sentenced by a judge in Tampa. He was transported to Marianna by Hillsborough County deputies to serve his time in the juvenile facility on July 6, 1945.

---

[94] Florida Industrial School Intake & Exit Ledger, Section 1945 & Section 1946.

Clarence had never served a long-term sentence, and as tough as he may have thought he was, "Marianna," as it was known to generations of teenagers across Florida, was a new level for him. The Industrial School resulted from a benevolent idea by Jackson County leaders at the end of the 19th century to create a place where a small number of children could be diverted from the harsh conditions of the chain gangs, cells, and predators of the Florida State Prison. The school would provide them with educational benefits and teach them trades so they could escape the cycle of poverty and crime. The state legislature gave them the school they sought but failed to provide much funding for such essentials as safe housing, food, medical care, staffing, and more. Then, judges across Florida poured students into the facility, swelling it far beyond its intended capacity. When administrators objected to small children – even infants – being sent there, one Tampa judge ordered that they produce a law showing him that he could not send anyone he desired to the school. There was no such law, and a facility intended for a small number of students soon housed hundreds. To make matters worse, the legislature expected it to cover almost all of its expenses, produce its food, build its buildings, and even generate a profit for the state when possible. After a horrible dormitory fire killed students and employees alike in 1914, the 1918 Spanish influenza swept through the campus – as it did through military camps, prisons, hospitals, and communities around the world. Once again, a high death rate and horrible conditions were reported.[95]

By the time Clarence Anglin arrived at the Florida Industrial School in 1945, most of the deaths of students there had already taken place. It was anything but the altruistic place envisioned by the people of Jackson County fifty years before. Life was tough for students, and discipline was rigid. Flogging was the standard punishment for escape attempts and serious rule infractions – as was the case at such facilities nationwide. Minor infractions could mean loss of privileges and "rank." Students who attended the school in the 1940s-1980s indicate that acts of physical

---

[95] Dale Cox, *Death at Dozier School*, Bascom: Old Kitchen Books, 2014.

violence and intimidation by older students were also not uncommon. The only recorded incidents of murder at the school were the result of student-on-student crime. The school's records also indicate that some staff members were disciplined for abuse against students. Likewise, written testimonials mailed to the school from former students reflect that other staff members treated students well. Clarence Anglin's name is not mentioned in the Florida Industrial School's disciplinary ledger that covers 1945-1946. If he had any such issues, they did not rise to the level of entering the school's records. He completed his legal sentence and was released to his mother on August 26, 1945.[96]

In other words, Clarence knew Marianna and – like many former students of its well-known juvenile facility – may not have had fond memories of his time there. And with that thought begins the story of the robbery of Marianna's Citizens State Bank on April 9, 1963:

MARIANNA – A $123,000 bank robbery here Tuesday probably provided Mariannans with more excitement than the town has had since its last lynching about 35 years ago.

Not since Union Brig. Gen. Alexander Asboth, with four battalions of cavalry and two companies of infantry came up from Pensacola to raid the place 99 years ago has so much been taken here at gunpoint. . . .

Taking part in the Tuesday's robbery, which showed evidences of better planning and generalship than Asboth provided his raiders, were only two bandits – plus a possible accomplice or two who managed to stay in the background.

The bandits, gloved, disguised and dressed as workmen, entered Citizen State Bank before opening hours through an employee entrance at the rear. After forcing bank officers and

---

[96] Florida Industrial School Intake & Exit Ledger, Section 1945 and Section 1946; Dale Cox, *Death at Dozier School*, Old Kitchen Books, 2014; Interviews with former students, Florida Industrial School and Dozier School for Boys, 1940s-1980s, Dozier School for Boys Files, D.R. Historic Preservation Archives; FBI, "Clarence Anglin," file no. 76-26295.

employees to lie on the floor, the robbers calmly took the money and fled in bank vice president Bowers Sandusky's car.[97]

Almost immediately, parallels were drawn between the heist and the robbery of the Bank of Jay. One of the robbers was around 5'8" tall. The other was tall and lean. Eyewitnesses varied in describing his height but placed it between 5'11" and 6'2". They agreed that he had light-colored or blonde hair. The shorter man had dark or black hair. In other words, they matched the descriptions of the Jay bank robbers. The Marianna witnesses noticed something else about the shorter man - and it was significant. He had a noticeable Creole accent.

The Pensacola police officer who became the focus of so much attention after the Bank of Jay robbery did not have a Creole accent, nor had he spent any significant time in Louisiana. On the other hand, Frank Lee Morris lived for many years in Louisiana and ranked New Orleans as his favorite city. He was 5'8", the same approximate height as the shorter of the robbers involved in both the Jay and Marianna incidents. He was also shorter than the other two escapees. Eyewitnesses said that the man with the Creole accent who helped rob Citizens Bank was shorter than the other two suspects.

"In 1963, I was working for Thrift Department Store located on Lafayette Street," explained Robert Earl Standland, who witnessed the robbery and briefly met the two robbers. He went to open the back door of the department store warehouse and latch its screen door on the morning of April 9 when he noticed someone in the back alley. "That morning before the robbery, I walked out the door, there was a gentleman out here looking," Standland explained while pointing out the location of events. "He asked me the question, did I know where the telephone line went to these buildings." Not realizing that he was speaking to a criminal, Standland tried to be helpful. "I said, 'Sure, we can follow them.'"

---

[97] E.W. Carswell, 'Not Since Civil War Has So Much Been Taken at Gunpoint in Marianna,' *Pensacola News-Journal*, April 14, 1963.

72

The original bank building in Marianna no longer stands, but Mr. Standland was able to point out its footprint and where he showed the bank robber how to access the phone lines leading to it and other businesses on the block:

> They have removed the bank building. . . When they went into the bank, they told Bowers Sandusky [bank president] to go get his car, give them the keys to his car, and he said he didn't drive his car that day, and they said 'yeah you did because we saw you drive and park it.' So they went and got his car, pulled the car through the drive-up, loaded the money – there was $100 and something thousand dollars they got – into Bowers Sandusky's car, left here, went to Alford, to Alford's dump site. . . left his car down there, they got in their car and disappeared. Nobody has ever found out who they were.[98]

Years passed, and John P. McDaniel became sheriff of Jackson County, but he was also on the scene of the Citizens Bank robbery of 1963. "I was in and out of there on a regular basis," he explained, "went in the back door and just walked down the hallway, and they would be in there getting set up and ready to go with the day's work." Many years after the robbery, McDaniel remembered warning bank president Bowers Sandusky that the unlocked back door was an open invitation for someone to rob the bank. Sandusky laughed him off. "Oh boy, that ain't gonna happen," Sandusky said. As McDaniel recalled, "It did." The retired sheriff remembered the day of the robbery sixty years after the fact:

> The day of the bank robbery, I happened to go by the bank at the time and I didn't see anything. At that

---

[98] Robert Earl Standland, Interview with author, December 14, 2018.

time I had gone out to the Caravan Restaurant, I know
they took Bowers Sandusky's car, and went south of
town off the Panama City cutoff, and went in there on
the Alford cutoff and hid it back in the woods. I think
they got it stuck back in there in the sand. That's about
all I know about that one.[99]

McDaniel's memories are consistent with reports given at the time.
The *Jackson County Floridan*, Marianna's now-defunct daily
newspaper, covered the crime with print and photographic reporting the
next day:

Two disguised gunmen Tuesday robbed the Citizens State
Bank in Marianna of an estimated $100,000 in cash, while bank
employes were forced at gunpoint to lie on the floor.

The robbery occurred about 8:20 a.m., 40 minutes before the
bank's business hours, and the gunmen fled in the car of Bowers
Sandusky, bank vice president. Sandusky's car was located at
11:26 a.m. three miles east of Alford near a garbage dump.

An intensive manhunt throughout Florida, Georgia, and
Alabama was instituted immediately and roadblocks were set up
within minutes by Florida Highway Patrol and sheriff's offices
in all neighboring counties. The search for the robbers is being
directed by agents of the Jacksonville district of the Federal
Bureau of Investigation, with cooperation of all local and state
law enforcement agencies.[100]

Marianna was a larger town than Columbia or Jay and the robbers,
in this case, came in through the back door instead of the front of the
bank. As the young future sheriff predicted, leaving it open proved to be

---

[99] Sheriff John P. McDaniel (Retired), Interview with author, December 15,
2018.
[100] "Citizens Bank Robbed Of $100,000," *The Jackson County Floridan*, April
10, 1963.

a vulnerability the robbers exploited. This demonstrates, as did Robert Earl Standland's recollection of two robbers searching for phone lines before the robbery, that the men had "cased" the building. This was yet another consistency with the Jay and Columbia robbery. The robbers at Jay had also tried to force an employee to pull the phone lines on their way out. In this case, they made sure that they knew how to do it themselves and did so as they made their way out the back door and piled into Sandusky's car.

Some differences between the Marianna robbery and the other two are worth noting. The Citizens State Bank heist occurred before the institution opened for the day instead of close to the lunch hour. The bandits also made a deliberate effort to disguise themselves. They wore coveralls and hard hats while pulling white bandanas across their faces. When he saw them without their faces covered, Robert Earl Standland thought they were from the phone company. They also stole a getaway car, using Bowers Sandusky's vehicle to escape to the so-called "sand pits" near Alford, where they had stashed another vehicle. How they got to Marianna from the location of the second car in the first place remains a mystery, but the technique of the escape was no different than that employed in the Jay robbery.

More information about the men and the car they were driving began to emerge during the 24 hours after the robbery:

> Officers Wednesday interviewed townspeople who were in the bank area as well as those on the highway near the site where the stole car was found.
>
> Several persons told officers they saw the men leave the bank and others told of seeing a car leaving the area at a high rate of speed.
>
> Information was volunteered that a 1954 dark colored Oldsmobile appeared to be following the get-away car and that three men were seen on several occasions before the robbery

parked across the street from the bank in a car answering the description of the Oldsmobile.[101]

Authorities determined that the robbers were not workers from the courthouse construction project across the street from the bank. The more officers looked into the robbery, the more impressed they became with the precision of it. One deputy thought that the culprits must have planned it for months because "every step they took looked like it was mapped out in advance."[102]

The focus was immediately on Officer L.J. Ingram and his fellow patrolman at the Pensacola Police Department because Chief D.P. Caldwell decided they had committed the robbery in Jay after seeing sketches of the suspects in the local newspaper. When the Bank of Jay executives failed to identify the second officer in a lineup, and the stacked lineup against Ingram fell apart, the attempt to link them to the holdup in Marianna collapsed as well. There simply was no evidence connecting the two police officers to either robbery.

Once the Pensacola Police theory fell apart, the FBI turned to Karl H. Close, a known bank robber. He was wanted for bank robberies in Baltimore, Maryland, and Roanoke, Virginia, when the FBI added him to its list of "10 Most Wanted." The Bureau also wanted not only Close but his brother, Harold, for questioning in connection with the Marianna and Jay robberies when authorities finally cornered and arrested him in South Carolina in September 1963:

> Close and his brother Harold were suspects in the $115,000 robbery of the Citizens State Bank of Marianna April 9.
>
> The FBI office in Jacksonville said Thursday night Karl Close will be questioned about the Marianna robbery and several others in Northwest Florida.

---

[101] "Investigation Continues As Every Clue Is Checked," *The Jackson County Floridan,"* April 11, 1963.
[102] *Ibid.*

A spokesman said the brothers are known to have been in Panama City, Destin and Tallahassee area about the time of the Panhandle robberies, but so far no definite connection has been established.[103]

No connection ever would be established between the Close brothers and the Marianna or Jay bank robberies. They didn't commit either crime. Ultimately, neither robbery was solved, and the criminals got away with more than $133,000 – well over $1,000,000 in today's dollars. Authorities recovered around $40,000. Perhaps *Pensacola News-Journal* writer E.W. Carswell was right when he wrote just days after the Citizen's State Bank robbery:

> The officers put a "remotely possible but highly improbable" tag on a suggestion that the robbery might have been committed by the Anglin brothers, Clarence and John, who joined bank robber Frank L. Morris of Louisiana in escaping from Alcatraz prison more than a year ago.
>
> Prison officials have reported having evidence that the men died while trying to cross San Francisco Bay on home-made rafts. But their bodies were never recovered.
>
> The Anglins, serving time for robbing the Columbia, Ala., bank of $25,000 in 1958, were natives of the Donalsonville, Ga., area. They are said to have been familiar with all of West Florida.[104]

Eyewitness Robert Earl Standlan was shown photographs of Clarence Anglin, John Anglin, and Frank Lee Morris. No wanted poster information was included, and he was not told that the possibility of a link between the Alcatraz escape and the bank robbery was being

---

[103] "'Most Wanted' Man Arrested," *Pensacola News-Journal.* September 27, 1963.
[104] E.W. Carswell, 'Not Since Civil War Has So Much Been Taken at Gunpoint in Marianna,' Pensacola News-Journal, April 14, 1963.

investigated. He immediately pointed to the photographs of John Anglin and Frank Morris and said, "It could be them."[105]

Historian Dale Cox believes robberies like the one at Citizens State Bank in Marianna in 1963 funded the Anglin brothers and Frank Morris's plan to leave the country. Inmates who knew them told investigators they planned to pull off one big heist and escape the United States. That was likely the plan for the Bank of Jay robbery and could explain how Alfred Anglin knew about it. If the prisoner in Atlanta was truthful in what he told FBI agents, Alfred was receiving messages from his brothers in a way that evaded the watchful eyes and ears of prison guards and the Federal Bureau of Investigation. In September 1963, Alfred was moved from Atlanta to Kilby Prison (now Kilby Correctional Facility) in Mt. Meigs near Montgomery, Alabama. A determination had been made that he could serve his state and federal sentences concurrently, so authorities transferred him to the Alabama state facility to continue his incarceration until he became eligible for parole. He told family members he knew where "the boys" were and could go to them. Without their knowledge, Alfred immediately developed a plan to do so.

---

[105] Standland, interview.

Chapter Eight

The Death of Alfred Anglin

One of the continuing mysteries about Alfred Ray Anglin, the third of the Anglin brothers, is whether and how the escapees communicated with him at the U.S. Penitentiary-Atlanta and Kilby Prison in Alabama. An inmate at the Leon County Jail in Tallahassee may have provided the answer. In an interview with the FBI, he said he knew a relative – either a first or second cousin – of Clarence and John Anglin, who "was bragging about having done jobs" with them. This relative was also serving time and had received a coded message in the form of a photograph of the family, including the brothers. "On the back of this picture was written," according to the FBI report, "The family is all well." The secret message was that everyone shown in the photograph was alive and well, including Clarence and John Anglin. The inmate believed that he could determine the location of the escapees in three days and find them in person within a few months.[106]

Interestingly, at least in documents released to the public by the FBI, agents did not connect this information to similar correspondence Alfred received from his family. He had received a presumably identical

---

[106] FBI Interview with Inmate at Leon County Jail, Name Redacted, November 18, 1963, included in Report of San Francisco Field Office, February 19, 1964, FBI, "Clarence Anglin," file no. 76-26295.

photograph, with a similar handwritten message on the back. Was the inmate in Tallahassee correct that this was a predetermined message that family members shared as a secret sign they had heard from "the boys"? If so, it explains how Alfred suddenly got word in the Atlanta federal prison that his brothers were alive and well when one of his brothers visited without guards realizing a message had been passed.[107]

By the summer of 1963, the media had moved on to other stories, and the Alcatraz escape slipped from front-page news to occasional mentions. The Federal Bureau of Investigation relentlessly worked on the case. Despite the claims of many modern writers that the Bureau wrote off the escapees as having drowned in San Francisco Bay or been swept to sea, agents across the country investigated reported sightings, tracked down acquaintances and family members, and followed up leads both reasonable and far-fetched. Even when some field offices would have preferred to let the investigation slip away, the San Francisco Special Agent-in-Charge kept pushing. There was enough belief in the possibility that Morris and the Anglins were successful to keep the search hot and heavy.

Alfred Anglin had served five years in the U.S. Penitentiary by 1963 and would be eligible for parole in another five years. He caused no trouble in Atlanta and had not attempted to escape, so authorities transferred him to state prison to finish the second half of his sentence. In September 1963, Alfred was transferred to Kilby Prison at Mt. Meigs near Montgomery, Alabama. Built in 1922-1923 on today's Kilby Correctional Facility site, the prison was massive. The reinforced concrete walls, which surrounded 27 acres, were 20 feet high and made of reinforced concrete. With a planned capacity of 900 convicts, the primary cell block featured five floors. On the top floor, inmates lived in single cells with private toilets and lavatories. The prison was modern for its day, with a hospital, power plant, laundry, kitchen, and dining

---

[107] Report of SAC San Francisco, April 15, 1964, FBI, "Clarence Anglin," file no. 76-26295.

halls. At least thirty bungalows outside the walls housed officials and employees. There was also a hotel for employees with families. The 2,500-acre reservation included a farm, dairy, cotton mill, shirt factory, and other operations. Prisoners were expected to be productive for the State of Alabama.[108]

When Alfred Anglin arrived at Kilby Prison in 1963, it was nearing the end of its long existence. The historic complex would be closed, demolished, and replaced just seven years later by the new Kilby Correctional Facility. Despite the aging structure and outdated facilities, Alfred initially seemed happy there. Perhaps it was just the change of pace after his years in federal prison, but he told family members that all was good. There is no indication in the official record that they knew he had an escape plan underway. Unfortunately for him, it did not go well:

> One of the notorious Anglin brothers was killed Saturday night as he attempted a daring escape from Kilby prison.
>
> Alfred Ray Anglin, 34, a convicted bank robber – whose two brothers escaped Alcatraz in 1962 and have not been heard from since – died when he was electrocuted.
>
> "Anglin cut the bars on a second-floor laundry room window with a hacksaw," prison commissioner Frank Lee said. "He had placed a rubber inner tube around the wire, but it wasn't enough protection."[109]

After allowing Alfred's relatives time to bury him and try to process their loss, FBI agents sat down with his parents and some siblings on January 27, 1964:

> They advised they were upset and it was obvious that they were emotionally disturbed over the recent death of ALFRED

---

[108] "History of the ADOC," Alabama Department of Corrections, accessed September 16, 2024, https://doc.alabama.gov/history.aspx.
[109] Charles Cates, "Alfred Anglin Electrocuted Trying to Flee From Kilby," *The Montgomery Advertiser*, January 12, 1964.

ANGLIN, and stated they had been contacted by a parole officer of the State of Florida, concerning the possible parole of ALFRED ANGLIN, who had been transferred from the Federal Penitentiary at Atlanta, Georgia, to Kilby Prison approximately September 18, 1963, to serve his state prison sentence of 25 years, while still serving the remainder of his Federal sentence concurrently. His mandatory release date was October 5, 1967, but he was to be under Federal supervision until August 13, 1972.[110]

The Anglins told FBI agents they last heard from Alfred via two letters. The first, written on Christmas day, "was cheerful and gave no indication of being restless." Some relatives had traveled to Kilby to visit him on December 22. He was optimistic that he would be granted parole soon and said he felt "free" after his years in Atlanta. Alfred Anglin's last contact with family was in a letter to one of his sisters that she received on New Year's Day, 1964. There was nothing unusual or distressing about the wording of the letter, but it was written on blue paper, which his relatives thought "could mean he was in solitary confinement." While at other facilities, he used colored paper to write them while being punished. There is no indication this was the case at Kilby.[111]

Alfred's family went on to explain to the FBI agents the difficulties they were having in obtaining his death certificate:

[They] continued that the family was notified at 11:30 PM, Saturday night, January 11, 1964, that ALFRED had been accidentally electrocuted at 8:30 PM that day while trying to escape from Kilby, and the family paid $283.00 to have the body returned to Ruskin for funeral services, and they stated they were

---

[110] Interview with Anglin Family, January 26, 1964, Report of SAC San Francisco Field Office, February 19, 1964, FBI, "Clarence Anglin," file no. 76-26295.
[111] *Ibid.*

further upset because no death certificate was received with the body, and although several attempts have been made by the funeral director to obtain a death certificate, it has not been forwarded by prison officials.[112]

FBI reports indicate that Bureau officials at the highest levels applied pressure to have the death certificate and any other requested documents expedited for the Anglin family.

The interview conducted by agents on January 27 also shows the extent to which the family was falling victim to different reports, rumors, and media accounts about what had happened to Alfred:

> ...[They] advised that a brother and sister of the ANGLINS had telephonically contacted Prison Chaplin [Redacted] who allegedly stated that ALFRED and another prisoner were on top of a prison building, when ALFRED became tangled in electric wire; that newspapers mentioned a window lined with high voltage wire, and further the family had also heard that the TV programs in Georgia had stated that ALFRED was sawing through the prison wall and had sawed through high voltage lines.
>
> [They] pointed out that in view of the above, they were not satisfied with the information they received. They said that they were upset because of the lack of knowledge of the fate of . . . CLARENCE and JOHN, in their attempted escape from Alcatraz, and this recent tragedy of . . . ALFRED. They also stated that they had heard through other members of the family that the funeral director at Ruskin had stated that the body was in bad shape and had "stripes" across his back and this caused them to wonder how ALFRED died.[113]

---

[112] *Ibid.*
[113] *Ibid.*

The confusion and emotional trauma caused trauma that events surrounding Alfred's death caused for members of the Anglin family continues to this day. The difficulty that they experienced in receiving a death certificate for him and the statements made to them by the funeral director from Lewers and Shannon Funeral Home in their hometown of Ruskin, Florida, raised suspicion and doubt that festered for a half-century. FBI records indicate that agents inquired into both issues. They learned from the funeral director at White Chapel Funeral Home in Montgomery that Kilby Prison only prepared death certificates once per month and that, three weeks after Alfred Anglin's death, the family should not expect to receive one for another "two or three weeks."[114]

Agents asked the funeral director in Ruskin about his observations of the condition of Alfred's body in an interview with him on January 27, 1964:

> ...[T]he body of ALFRED ANGLIN showed no indication of mistreatment, but had two small burned areas on the upper back and burned areas above each eye and bridge of nose, possibly from electric current going through eyeglasses. He stated that although glasses were not sent to him with the body, ALFRED ANGLIN allegedly wore glasses all the time. He said that ALFRED had an abrasion on the right cheek and the lower right abdomen, possibly caused by a scrape against concrete, and the only complaint he had concerning the condition of the body was a complaint over inferior embalming and restorative work by the funeral parlor in Montgomery, Alabama, which he mentioned to relatives, and made no open complaint.[115]

---

[114] Report of SAC San Francisco Field Office, February 19, 1964, FBI, "Clarence Anglin," file no. 76-26295.
[115] FBI Interview with Funeral Director, Lewers and Shannon Funeral Home, Ruskin, Florida, January 26, 1964, Report of SAC San Francisco Field Office, February 19, 1964, FBI, "Clarence Anglin," file no. 76-26295.

The funeral director did not explain to agents why – or if – he might have made different statements to members of the Anglin family than he did to them. The parents and siblings of Alfred firmly believed that he gave them information that indicated their family member had suffered from abuse and a likely suspicious death. So concerned were they that the U.S. Department of Justice opened a Civil Rights Investigation into the matter. The final report of this inquiry was submitted on March 31, 1964, and summarized the information previously gathered by FBI agents. The report also included new information on the escape attempt that led to Alfred's death:

> On the night of January 11, 1964, at approximately 6:30 p.m., ANGLIN, along with inmate ALTHEA SENN gained entrance to and secluded themselves in the institution's clothing room on the second floor at Kilby Prison. At approximately 8:00 p.m. that date, the indicator in the lobby at the prison indicated a ground on the high tension security wires surrounding the compound. Investigation revealed inmate SENN attempting to attract the attention of a guard on that floor. When the guard approached, SENN told him that ANGLIN had come in contact with the electric wire outside the window. Examination revealed that two window bars had been sawed at the bottom and were bent upward, which had been done by a piece of 1½" water pipe as a bender. A protective screen on the outside of the bars was also sawed through. ANGLIN was completely through the window with the exception of his feet. The inmate's face and body were lying on the flat roof of the Administration Offices and his feet were still in the hole in the window when he came in contact with the high voltage security wire, thereby electrocuting himself.[116]

---

[116] "Alfred Ray Anglin: Civil Rights," Tampa, Florida, March 31, 1964, Federal Bureau of Investigation, U.S. Department of Justice.

A search of Senn, Anglin's body, and the surrounding area produced a hacksaw in a "crudely made frame," a pair of wire pliers, two sets of jumper wires that the inmates planned to use for hotwiring automobiles, a forged Alabama Driver's License, and $16 in cash. A waterproof package of personal photographs and a list of addresses, including local names and some from across several states, was also found.[117]

The investigation determined that "Anglin's clothing had become entangled on a portion of the window." FBI Agents learned from their interviews and reviews of prison records that "In bending and twisting in an attempt to release his clothing, he raised up too high, coming in contact with the wire at a point about the middle of his back, thus causing his death." Alfred's body was carried from the scene to the Kilby Prison Hospital:

> Following his death, the coroner at Montgomery, Alabama, was immediately notified of it. An examination was made by the coroner and a death certificate was filled out at the hospital, Kilby Prison, which certificate was sent to the coroner for his signature. As it is normally the case, the death certificate was forwarded by the coroner to Alabama Bureau of Vital Statistics, Montgomery, Alabama. A record of death was then filed with Alabama Bureau of Vital Statistics and is on record. A death certificate is not in possession of Kilby Prison Officials and would not in this case or any case be forwarded to the family of ANGLIN and if the family of ANGLIN desire a certificate of death, it was felt they could obtain one by contact with the Alabama Bureau of Vital Statistics, Department of Health, Montgomery Alabama.[118]

Once again, the Anglin family had been misinformed by others about the information regarding their loved one – in this case, the death

---

[117] *Ibid.*
[118] *Ibid.*

certificate for Alfred for which they had been waiting – and were in financial difficulty because they needed it to file an insurance claim to cover his burial expenses. The changing story about how to obtain a death certificate and what the funeral director said about suspicious marks on Alfred's body added more to the hard times the family was experiencing. Siblings of the three Anglin brothers told FBI agents that "their elderly parents, especially their father, had suffered so much in the mystery of losing JOHN WILLIAM and CLARENCE that they doubted the parents will ever accept or understand the truth surrounding the death of ALFRED."[119]

The remaining Anglin brothers and sisters who spoke to the FBI in 1964 were correct. The family never accepted the official report on Alfred's death. The incident surged back before the public eye in a gruesome and headline-grabbing way in 2020. Alfred was exhumed – in full color for the world to see – as part of a documentary aired on The History Channel. David Widner – nephew of Alfred, John, and Clarence – told the *Albany Herald* that he and other family members agreed to participate because they believed that Alfred was beaten to death at Kilby Prison. He described a "family meeting" that took place at a picnic table on the prison grounds a few days before the alleged electrocution. This refers to the prison visit made by Anglin family members to Alfred at Kilby on Sunday, December 22, 1963. It is understandable how members of the family could reach such a conclusion since the funeral director in 1964 told them that Alfred had "stripes" across his back.[120]

The documentary did not make a breakthrough in the case of Alfred Anglin, despite the shocking use of footage of Alfred's embalmed body straight from the grave after nearly 60 years. A new examination by 21st-

---

[119] *Ibid.*

[120] Carlton Fletcher, "Georgia nephew of famed prison escapees keeps their story alive decades later," *Albany Herald*, June 23, 2020, Updated May 18, 2022, accessed October 1, 2024, https://www.albanyherald.com/features/georgia-nephew-of-famed-prison-escapees-keeps-their-story-alive-decades-later/.

century medical examiners proved only that he was not beaten to death at Kilby prison. The autopsy determined that he died from the effects of electrocution.

David and Ken Widner also provided DNA to test human bones found at San Francisco Bay about one-half year after the Alcatraz escape. They were not a match for the Anglin brothers. The media played this up a bit as breaking news, but the FBI had submitted the remains to the coroner in San Francisco at the time they were discovered. The determination then was that the measurements were inconsistent with any of the three escapees. Ultimately, the forensic investigations confirmed what was already known.[121]

---

[121] FBI, "Clarence Anglin," file no. 76-26295.

Chapter Nine

Mexico, the Bahamas, Brazil, and Colombia

Historian Dale Cox believes the 1963 Citizens State Bank robbery in Marianna funded the Anglin brothers' and Frank Morris' plans to settle outside the country. The question is, where did they go? The inmate who shared a cell with their brother Alfred at the U.S. Penitentiary in Atlanta thought they would make for Mexico:

> [He] advised that if he were to start looking for the Subjects, he would start looking in the vicinity of Guadalajara, Mexico, in that Subject MORRIS, who speaks fluent Spanish, spent a great deal of time in that area from 1953 to 1957. He stated MORRIS has a lot of contacts in that area, and that if the Subjects were alive, as he believes, MORRIS would be "calling the shots," and in all probability would be "holed up" in that area. He explained that the Subjects were all excellent woodsmen and would think nothing of "holing up" in the Guadalajara Mountain Range for years.[122]

---

[122] FBI Interview at USP-Atlanta, February 28, 1964, SAC Report, San Francisco Field Office, April 15, 1964, FBI, "Clarence Anglin," file no. 76-26295.

The inmate provided FBI agents with the name of a close friend of Frank Lee Morris, who lived in Guadalajara or Monterrey, Mexico. The two cities are about 490 miles apart, with mountains near both. He told them that the individual he named would help Morris and the Anglins or at least be aware if they were in the area, "but would not cooperate with any law enforcement agency."[123]

The inmate also mentioned that Alfred Anglin hid out for five years around "Haynes, Florida," when he escaped from state custody, but said he had "no reason to believe" the Alcatraz escapees would go there. FBI agents either misspelled Haines City in their report or never bothered to check out the possibility that the escapees were hiding in "Haynes," a rural community in Jackson County, Florida. Haines City, where Alfred hid, is located in Polk County, near Lakeland. Clarence went there, too, on at least one occasion after escaping from a road camp near Fort Myers, thanks to help from his older brother Robert. There is no evidence in the public FBI file to suggest that the FBI looked for the escapees in the Haines City (or Haynes) area, likely because Alfred had died at Kilby Prison before the tip was received. If the latter man had received information that the other three were hiding somewhere familiar, the Central Florida community would have been a good place to start looking.[124]

Evidence shows that the escapees may have spent some of their time in 1962-1965 just sixty-four miles off the Florida coast on Grand Bahama Island. According to author Peter Wohlfelder, who wrote *Alcatraz: Escapees in the Bahamas*, three American strangers matching the descriptions of Frank Morris, John Anglin, and Clarence Anglin appeared on Grand Bahama around 1962 and remained there for several years. Many Americans escape to the Bahamas today. The islands are

---

[123] *Ibid.*

[124] *Ibid.*; Michael Essliger and David Widner, *Escaping Alcatraz: The Untold Story of the Greatest Prison Break in American History*, San Francisco: Ocean View Publishing, 2023.

full of beaches, resorts, and tourist attractions. Grand Bahama, though, was very remote in the early 1960s. The three mysterious men settled in an isolated home in the bush at the far southeast end of the island.[125]

According to Wohlfelder, a Bahamian named Freddie Pinder remembered how he went to live with his aunt on Grand Bahama in June 1962 after the unfortunate death of his mother the previous month. He was only five years old at the time. The three Americans appeared soon after, living in a hidden spot behind his aunt's farm. They came seeking water and food in the months following their arrival, but residents showed kindness and helped them. The strangers disappeared from Grand Bahama around 1965. The U.S. Marshals Service recently investigated a claim that Clarence Anglin died on another island in the Bahamas. Fingerprint examination showed that the man in question was not Anglin, but the stories of their presence on Grand Bahama in the early 60s are enigmatic. Wohlfelder's book is a fascinating read that raises questions left unanswered by U.S. authorities.[126]

FBI agents, meanwhile, continued to watch for any sign of the escapees in the United States. Family members, acquaintances, and those who had served time in prison with the men were interviewed and reinterviewed. Surveillance was maintained, and leads were followed. Two heavily redacted teletypes in the files released to the public by the Bureau also indicate that the investigation was spreading overseas, particularly to Brazil. The country had no extradition treaty with the United States before December 17, 1964. In roughly one month after the treaty went into effect, allowing fugitives to be extradited to the U.S., 16 of 18 wanted American criminals in Brazil had been located and were being returned home.[127]

---

[125] Peter Wohlfelder, *Alcatraz: Escape to the Bahamas*, Bloomington: AuthorHouse: Updated Edition, June 19, 2017.
[126] *Ibid.*
[127] Legat, Rio de Janeiro to Director, FBI, January 20, 1965, FBI, "Clarence Anglin," file no. 76-26295.

The two teletypes are so heavily redacted that all that can be determined from them is that U.S. authorities in Brazil arrested a fugitive who had been living in the country for three years. The man had obtained a U.S. passport under a false name, "had entered Brazil under that name, had obtained his permanent visa under that name, had brought his wife into the country," and would have become a naturalized citizen within a few days had he not been located. One of the teletypes lists Frank Morris as its subject, while the other lists Clarence Anglin as the subject. There is not one in the publicly available documents for John Anglin. The teletypes demonstrate how easily the escapees could have obtained fake passports and escaped the United States. They also show that the FBI had received information that Morris and Clarence Anglin "might be living in the Rio de Janeiro area" under assumed names. No trace of them was found in 1965, but the story of a connection between the escapees and Brazil was far from over.[128]

In 2015, The History Channel released a 40-year-old photograph of two men standing by an enormous termite mound. The alleged photographer was a former drug smuggler named Fred Brizzi, Jr. He gave it to the Anglin family in the early 1990s, claiming that it was taken in Brazil in 1975. The media reported that the men in it were said by Brizzi to be Clarence and John Anglin. Historian Dale Cox is open-minded about the photograph. "I don't necessarily believe that the photograph is of the Anglin Brothers," he says, shrugging his shoulders, "Might be. Might not." He notes that one expert says it very well could be the Anglin brothers due to facial point matches, but another says the arms of the men in the photo are too long. "I don't know," he concludes, "I am not an expert on such things."

To better understand the photograph's reliability, the authors submitted it to law enforcement experts for another review. Their first comment was a warning that any forensic examination of photographic evidence originating from a film negative should be conducted using the

---

[128] *Ibid.*

original negative, rather than a print or reprint of unknown quality. The printing process can exaggerate dimensions from the negative if the person making the prints is not an expert in their craft. Even slight changes in facial dimensions can lead to incorrect measurements, which may result in false positives or negatives when comparing photographs to known images of a subject. In other words, comparing the Brizzi photograph with a high level of forensic accuracy to different pictures of the Anglin brothers was impossible.

Considering this warning, we consulted law enforcement experts to examine the photograph anyway. They used a technique that compares different parts of the face between two images to identify clear matches. The results were inconclusive. The man on the left in the Brizzi photograph – purported to be Clarence Anglin – was so obscured by a beard and sunglasses that it was impossible to compare him with other known images of the escapees. The man on the right in the Brizzi photograph – purported to be John Anglin – was a somewhat closer match to known photos of him. The experts we consulted were only willing to say that "the odds were more likely than not" that the man on the right in the Brizzi image was John William Anglin. However, they also firmly cautioned that they did not consider the single print made available thus far "sufficient for a conclusive determination of identity" without examining the original negative. They were also unwilling to estimate the odds that the man on the left was Clarence Anglin, simply stating that the photograph did not provide the necessary detail for an accurate examination.

The analysis commissioned for this history was underwhelming. The photograph was of insufficient quality to compare the two men shown in it to the Anglin brothers. Only after that fact was clearly stated were the law enforcement experts who reviewed it for us even willing to guess that one of the men was "slightly better than a 50-percent match" to John Anglin. They were unwilling to compare the other individual to Clarence Anglin.[129]

---

[129] "Comparison Analysis of Purported Anglin Photograph," July 17, 2024.

Perhaps there is a reason that the photograph was insufficient for comparison. Fred Brizzi, in fact, never claimed that it was of the Anglin brothers. The lifelong "con man" told members of the Anglin family that he knew John and Clarence in their younger days. He claimed he ran into them at a bar in Rio de Janeiro in 1975. The old acquaintances struck up a conversation, and – according to Brizzi's statements – they took him to a ranch they owned in a rural area far from Rio. They showed him their home and cattle and even took him bodysurfing in a local lake. He waited nearly 20 years to tell the Anglin family about this experience, only coming forward to them after a long and less-than-stellar criminal career. He produced a set of photographs – including one with two men standing by a large termite mound – as evidence of the time he claimed to have spent with the brothers in Brazil. The other photos show a home, which he said was the ranch house of the Anglin brothers, a lake, and other highlights of the country around a small Brazilian town. Only in 2024, however, did nephew Ken Widner and writer Mike Lynch disclose that Brizzi actually did not tell the Anglin family that the photograph of two men and an ant mound was of the missing escapees.[130]

When the photograph of the alleged escapees was released, it generated worldwide publicity and was hailed as a "game-changer" in the search for proof that they had survived. How could this have happened if Brizzi never claimed it showed the Anglin brothers? According to Widner and Lynch, the entire idea that it was of the brothers was conceived by Anglin family members years after they met with Fred Brizzi. They were reviewing the photographs he had given them when they noticed that the two men shown standing by a termite mound resembled Clarence and John. The History Channel and worldwide media generated a sensation over the photo, with some stories even going so far as to state that Brizzi took it as a favor so the family would know that the men were well. Brizzi, however, never claimed that it showed

---

[130] Ken Widner and Mike Lynch, *Alcatraz: The Final Escape*, Lyons Press, 2024.

the Anglin brothers, and definitely never said he took the image to provide proof of life to the family.[131]

Fred Brizzi did live a colorful and often criminal life. He was involved in drug smuggling from South America into the United States in 1975, the year in which he claimed to have met John and Clarence Anglin in Brazil. That country, however, was not the center for drug flights making their way across the Atlantic and Gulf to the United States in 1975. The center for that activity was Colombia. And the destination for a vast number of those flights was Florida. The Sunshine State was such a center for arriving drug planes in the 1970s that they seemed to be popping up everywhere. In Englewood, just 60 miles from the home of the Anglin family in Ruskin, for example, residents welcomed the year 1975 with frustrations over the fact that a wrecked drug smuggler's plane sat resting on the tropical shore just outside their beachfront bungalows. The twin-engine Beechcraft crash-landed "a few hundred yards north of the county beach" the previous November while bringing in a load of marijuana. Owner Robert Glenn Evans of Fort Lauderdale had not appeared to remove it six weeks after the crash, and the homeowners were tired of looking at it.[132]

The headlines became more prominent as the planes got bigger. By August 1975, newspapers across the Southeast reported that a Fort Lauderdale man was one of thirteen suspects charged in a smuggling operation that flew a vintage World War II-era DC-4 across the Gulf and landed it at Treat Mountain in western Georgia. The pilot brought the plane in over Northwest Florida and flew straight up the Chattahoochee River valley to land it on a 600-foot runway that had been cleared using bulldozers during the hours preceding his arrival. A state helicopter pilot accustomed to flying low through the mountains was amazed by the pinpoint accuracy of the night landing. Law enforcement seized 3,200

---

[131] *Ibid.*
[132] "Wrecked Drug Plane Vexes Citizens," *Charlotte News-Press*, January 10, 1975.

pounds of marijuana, 75 pounds of hashish, and $180,000 in cash, but estimated that they got only half the load.[133]

As the decade drew to a close, the operations were so significant in scale that smugglers could afford to abandon a DC-6B, a four-engine aircraft, on a former military airstrip in Jackson County, Florida. Eight tons of marijuana were offloaded from the plane, local phone lines were cut, and two locals came closer than they ever knew to losing their lives. They appeared at the airstrip just minutes before the pilot brought the DC-6B in for a night landing, but fortunately left before the waiting ground crew could confront them. One of the leaders of the smuggling operation later testified in federal court that the marijuana was sold for $270 a pound, a price that would have generated $2,160,000. Local citizens charged in the operation ranged from a game warden and an auto dealership manager to a crop duster pilot and an aircraft mechanic. These were just the lower-level people, though, and there were much more prominent and wealthier individuals higher up the chain. Some of the locals were convicted. Some were found not guilty. The arrests did nothing to dampen the drug flights into Florida.[134]

The Jackson County DC-6B landing occurred five years after Fred Brizzi allegedly took the photograph of Anglin in 1975, but similar smuggling was widespread at the time. Charles F. Etheridge, Sr, the alleged American ringleader of the Jackson County operation, allegedly flew in multiple loads of drugs before the DC-6B shipment. The South American country of Colombia was the center point of such shipments to the United States in the 1970s, not Brazil. Drug movement from Brazil was more in the form of cocaine, and it was usually done by boat through Mexico and from there to the U.S. The flights – including those in which Brizzi was involved – took off mostly from Colombia.

---

[133] Robert Retchko, "Local Man Jailed, Another Sought In $1 Million Drug Plane Seizure," *Fort Lauderdale News*, August 6, 1975.

[134] Bob Sanford, "Bonds set in drug case," *Jackson County Floridan*, August 13, 1980; Bob Sanford, "Etheridges Tell About Landing DC-6 Loaded With Marijuana," *Jackson County Floridan*, November 13, 1980.

It was at the time of Brizzi's alleged meeting with the Anglin brothers that the drug smuggling business gained a new face. Pablo Escobar, the leader of the Medellin Cartel, surged to power in Colombia. While the marijuana shipments continued to fly, he built his criminal empire on America's sudden demand for cocaine. Thanks to media glamorization and widespread availability provided by the Medellín Cartel, cocaine became the indispensable party drug of the late 1970s. Columbia was the world's capital for its production. Anyone from America smuggling, buying, selling, or using drugs from 1975 to 1980, more likely than not, was enriching Pablo Escobar.

Fred Brizzi was in South America when he claimed, but documentation indicates that his smuggling flights originated from Colombia and the Bahamas. The FBI looked in Brazil on multiple occasions but never found a trace of the escapees. The case file, however, shows that agents never searched for the brothers in Colombia. The photo that Brizzi gave to the Anglin family shows two men posing by a large termite mound. There are such mounds in Colombia. The Medellin and later Cali Cartels controlled much of the country in the 1970s and 1980s, making it a prime destination for smugglers like Fred Brizzi. They moved plane loads of marijuana and cocaine across the water to Florida – flying in low to avoid detection and landing in isolated spots from the Everglades to the Panhandle. Massive drug shipments came in all around the Wiregrass area that the Anglin brothers had once called home.

Despite how he represented himself in later years, Fred Brizzi was not a particularly successful smuggler. In a "dumbest criminals" move, he left receipts for fuel with his name on them in a drug plane. To make the situation worse, the aircraft was blasted from the sky not by the DEA or U.S. Coast Guard but by a World War ll veteran with a shotgun. The recovery of the fuel receipts led to Brizzi's arrest. He found himself in serious trouble with federal authorities. He started making deals. He turned on associates and squealed on anyone and everyone that he could to avoid a lengthy prison sentence. Through it all, even as he turned in his best friends, Fred Brizzi never mentioned knowing anything about the Alcatraz escapees. The federal government found nothing in his effects to suggest a connection to the Anglin brothers. When he desperately turned in dangerous characters to lessen his time in jail, Fred Brizzi never mentioned to anyone that the long-sought Alcatraz escapees were living the good life on a ranch in Brazil. Turning on participants in drug smuggling operations – in fact, even being a snitch at all – held the danger of dramatically shortening his life either in prison or on the streets. He was neither a best friend nor a family member of John and Clarence Anglin. In fact, by 1975, when he claimed to have met them in Rio, the men had been off the radar for thirteen years. And since they had been imprisoned before the escape for four years, at least seventeen years had passed since Brizzi would have seen either of them. If he had proof that they were alive, why did he not turn it to his advantage? Snitching on the Anglin brothers would have been far less dangerous than snitching on drug smugglers.

His ex-wife probably thought the same thing when reporters confronted her in 2015 about the alleged photograph of the Anglin brothers. She told the media that she remembered the photo in question but never associated it with the Alcatraz escape, nor did Fred make any claims about the men shown in it. According to her, Brizzi told her he was amazed by the size of the termite mound and took the photograph to show her. In other words, the mound was the photo's focus, not the two men standing beside it. They were included for scale to show the size of the mound. She said that her ex-husband never mentioned anything about the men, other than that she could see how massive the termite mound was by how high it stood next to them. She did not recall him ever mentioning the Anglin brothers. The ex, who lived with him during his smuggling years, told journalists that Fred Brizzi was a "conman."[135]

Brizzi's ex-wife's statements that the photograph was of a termite mound, not the men pictured with it, never received widespread publicity. Her memories, however, combine with the Anglin family's

---

[135] Paul Thompson, ."EXCLUSIVE: 'In all the years we were together he never talked about those men' - Widow of drug smuggler who claimed he ran into the Alcatraz escapees in Brazil says husband was a 'con artist'," *Daily Mail*, October 16, 2015.

disclosure that the former criminal never told them the photo was of the missing brothers to raise serious doubts about its validity as evidence in the case. An independent analysis for this book and an assessment by the U.S. Marshals Service raises questions about whether the image can be used to identify anyone, let alone the missing Alcatraz escapees.

If Brizzi had met with John and Clarence Anglin, and they were living open lives – albeit with false names – on a ranch in Brazil, they would have been reasonably easy to find. The opposite has been the case. Multiple researchers have gone to Brazil to investigate the claim. Visits to the community where he claimed their ranch was located yielded nothing. No one remembered the American escapees. No evidence was found to suggest that they ever owned a ranch in that area. The local sheriff recalled that some Americans camped in a nearby cave. A brief investigation revealed some evidence of a camp, including a 1950s U.S. penny, but nothing significant to the case was found. One penny from a cave is far from proof that the Alcatraz escapees ever lived in the community, especially if, as one family member claims, they married, had children, and were the patriarchs of large families. No children, grandchildren, spouses, or other relatives of the men were found.

Ken Widner and Mike Lynch claimed in 2014 that Robert Anglin, Clarence and John's older brother, flew down and spent time with the escapees on their ranch. No evidence to support this claim has been produced. Another nephew, David Widner, indicated in a solid book of his own that his uncle Robert made a dying declaration that the brothers were alive and that he had been with them. The account included no claims as to where Robert might have seen his brothers, but it does mention that he moved away from his family and lived in Texas for a time. Robert is also the family member who informed Alfred Anglin in 1962 that the escape was successful. FBI interviews indicate that after seeing him, Alfred told his cellmate that he knew where the "boys" were and could go to them. Unfortunately, Robert took the details with him when he passed away. No concrete evidence has been presented to suggest that he mentioned or traveled to Brazil. The U.S. Marshals Service can access passport and visa records, but has never confirmed any travel from the U.S. to Brazil by Robert or other Anglin family members in the 1960s-1980s.

None of this means that the escapees were not in Brazil. Clearing up details of the Brizzi story, especially that he never claimed the photograph given to the family was of the missing men, removes what many consider solid proof that the Alcatraz escape succeeded. Brizzi should still be regarded as a possible witness, and he did produce photographs to verify that he was in Brazil at some point. In the end, however, there is no evidence that the widely published photograph of two men and a termite mound was ever taken as proof that the Anglin brothers were alive and well.

So, what evidence exists that the Anglin brothers survived and were in South America? In addition to Fred Brizzi, others involved in the drug smuggling business claimed to have seen them there. Those claims center around Colombia, not Brazil, and come from individuals once engaged in the serious smuggling of illegal drugs into the United States. They allege that they knew the escapees and saw them in Colombia. The story emerged after the Alcatraz investigation gained momentum again in the late 1980s. And after a relative of the Anglins told deputy marshals that at least two of the missing men were back in Florida.

Chapter Ten

Greenwood, Florida

THE U.S. MARSHALS SERVICE MAINTAINS an active investigation into the Alcatraz escape to this day. That is how historian Dale Cox, co-author of this book, found himself on the trail of the escapees in the 1980s. It all started some twenty-five years after the three men pushed off in their handmade inflatable raft:

> I was a reporter at WJHG-TV, that is a television station in Panama City, Florida, back in the 1980s, and I happened to be making rounds in a small town called Marianna, Florida. In the process of making those rounds, the sheriff casually mentioned to me that the U.S. Marshals were in town. It is always kind of interesting when the marshals are up to something and so I asked him, "What are they up to?" And he said, "Well, they are investigating something to do with the Alcatraz escape." Like most people, what I knew about the Alcatraz escape at that time was Clint Eastwood's movie 'Escape from Alcatraz.'[136]

---

[136] Dale Cox, Interview with author, July 6, 2018.

John P. McDaniel was the sheriff of Jackson County, Florida, at the time. He and Cox went to visit the U.S. Marshal in Tallahassee:

> And we met with U.S. Marshal Mac McClendon, who I remember very well because he was a big John Wayne fan. After the Unsolved Mysteries broadcast about the Escape from Alcatraz, the U.S. Marshals Service had posted a number and anyone who had information was asked to call into that number. And a woman who identified herself only as "Cathy" called in. She then went into details about how they escaped from Alcatraz. And what she said was that they did make it to shore, that a former sheriff from Florida, who was a relative of hers, had gone there and helped them, had picked them up and brought them back to this region of the country.[137]

Deputy U.S. marshals began their investigation at Greenwood within days of NBC's airing an "Unsolved Mysteries" program about the escape on February 8, 1989. A woman named "Cathy" phoned the toll-free number promoted during the program and provided specific, actionable information about two Alcatraz escapees. As it unfolded, her story was that she had often visited relatives in the farming country just northwest of Greenwood, Florida. While there, she occasionally stopped by a nearby home where two men lived. One of them was Clarence Anglin. The other one she thought might be Frank Morris, based on an aged sketch of him that NBC producers included in the program.[138]

Cathy's statements were investigated, and deputy marshals quickly learned she was related to Clarence and John Anglin. Her extended family included many members who were living in Jackson County and neighboring Houston County, Alabama, where the Anglin brothers

---

[137] *Ibid.*
[138] FBI, "Clarence Anglin," file no. 76-26295.

102

robbed the Bank of Columbia. One of her relatives, as she claimed, had been the sheriff of Jackson County decades earlier. Then, she dropped a bombshell. According to Cathy, the escapees had been helped by members of the Ku Klux Klan. Further check of her family tree revealed not only that she had relatives who were known KKK members, but one was convicted for his involvement in the infamous Birmingham Church Bombing of 1963.[139]

The Ku Klux Klan is no longer a factor in daily life in the Wiregrass area, thanks in large part to diligent efforts by law enforcement leaders and officers to stamp out criminal activity involving the organization's members. The situation, however, was different in the 1960s when Clarence Anglin, John Anglin, and Frank Morris escaped Alcatraz. The Anglin brothers had distant relatives involved in the Klan during its heyday, a time when the group was active and feared across large swaths of the country. There is no doubt that members of white supremacist organizations, including the KKK, were incarcerated at Alcatraz in the 1950s-1960s. Frank Morris even had a blue star tattooed on his forehead at one point in his life, but he removed it by the time of his Alcatraz incarceration. Blue star tattoos often indicate that inmates have served previous time in prison. Displayed in such a prominent place as the forehead, however, they can also signify membership in white supremacist prison gangs. Prison records leave no doubt that Allen Clayton West, the inmate who did not make it out of Alcatraz with Morris and the Anglins, had strong white supremacist leanings.[140]

Cathy's story checked so many boxes for deputy marshals that additional resources were applied to the investigation as a direct result of her statements. A review of the FBI escape file showed that the Bureau maintained contact with and sometimes visited other relatives of the Anglin brothers in several nearby communities, including the larger city of Dothan, Alabama. Investigators also noted that Donalsonville, the

---

[139] Ibid.

[140] Various newspaper articles describing law enforcement interactions with the Klan in the Wiregrass area, 1960-2024; FBI, "Clarence Anglin," file no. 76-26295.

birthplace of the Anglins, was just across the Chattahoochee River in Seminole County, Georgia. Donalsonville is within just a few miles of their childhood home in southern Early County. Excitement grew as a believable story clicked into place. The probability that at least one of the brothers might be hiding in plain sight in Greenwood generated considerable buzz in the law enforcement community.

Cathy mentioned that a man she believed could be Frank Lee Morris was living with Clarence in Greenwood, which also intrigued deputy marshals. It was not the first time a man thought to be Morris was spotted in the Southeast since the escape. In 1967, a man named Frankie Lyons reappeared in the French Quarter of New Orleans. Frankie was well known in the Crescent City. He was also well known to the FBI. Frankie Lyons was the alias of Frank Lee Morris. It did not take long for Frankie's presence in New Orleans to reach FBI agents investigating the Alcatraz escape. They spread out into the old city, visiting bars and nightclubs on the government dime, but Frankie again vanished into the mists from which he appeared. The night people saw him, even as the FBI looked for him, but the government agents never seemed to be in the right clubs at the right time to catch up with him. New Orleans is just that kind of place. It was mainly in the 1960s, when the Dixie Mafia was in control, that individuals like Frank Lee Morris could come and go, and the denizens of the dark enjoyed pulling one over on J. Edgar's boys. The trail went cold, but not before the FBI invested significant time and effort in the New Orleans investigation. FBI files show that multiple agents repeatedly attempted to corner Morris in New Orleans but failed.

Dale Cox recalls more of the story that Cathy told the U.S. Marshals Service:

> She basically told a story that they lived near her uncle, and that she had met them as she was coming back home to Jackson County, Florida, to the little community of Greenwood to visit family. She knew Clarence Anglin. . . The other person there, she believed to be Frank Morris. They were living and basically

doing farm work, which was a common occupation here in those days. [She said] that they had been there for a good while. . . she had visited them on several occasions. She was the one who gave this description of a brick house, with a pole barn behind it, on a specific road outside of Greenwood.

The investigation in Jackson County started to go sideways when the deputy marshals brought "Cathy" to the little town of Greenwood, Florida. They asked her to show them the house; Cox was privy to what happened next:

> The U.S. Marshals wanted "Cathy" to take them to this place, and during all of this process "Cathy" came and then suddenly acted confused like she didn't know where to go. And then she admitted to them that her family had told her to shut up – and in no uncertain terms to shut up. It was apparently at about the point that her family told her to be quiet that the two men who were living in this home disappeared.

Cathy, who had told such a straightforward story to deputy marshals before arriving with them in Greenwood, lost all memory of the house where she had seen the men. Investigators searched in vain for the location she described to them earlier. Cox, however, was familiar with the area, having grown up nearby. He attended high school in Malone, a community just six miles north of Greenwood, and even knew some of her distant relatives. He could direct investigators to the correct road and farm that Cathy had described, but claimed to have forgotten.

The home identified by the informant, Cathy, as the one where Clarence Anglin and possibly Frank Lee Morris lived stood just over 2 miles northwest of Greenwood. It was a single-story brick house with a pole barn behind it. The relatives she visited lived in the house north of it, and although they owned their property, the house where she alleged the two escapees lived was rented from a large farming operation.

Ownership of all of the land in the vicinity has changed since 1989. No trace of the house she described remains today. It was destroyed, and the site was converted to agricultural use between 1989 and 2012. It can be seen in historical aerial photographs on file at the University of Florida, along with a prominent tree in the yard. The tree is also gone.[141]

Deputy marshals and county law enforcement visited the home in 1989 but found that the two men described by Cathy were no longer there. Her relatives still lived just up the road but denied any knowledge about the Alcatraz escapees or their family's alleged involvement in hiding them. Other sources indicated that two men matching the descriptions of those provided by the woman did live in the target home but had recently moved out. Did they flee after news spread through the family that Cathy had reported them? That question remains open. Law enforcement officers were both intrigued and frustrated by her story. She told it well and included so many verifiable facts – and revealed previously unknown connections between her family and the Anglin family – that investigators remain deeply curious today. U.S. Marshal Mac McClendon said in 1991 that the information was "too precise for us to ignore." Major John Dennis (retired) of the Jackson County Sheriff's Department said at the time, "I first thought there was no way those boys could be alive. But, you know, you begin looking at it… I think they may have escaped."[142]

Major Dennis came away from the investigation convinced that at least two of the escapees – Clarence Anglin and Frank Morris – were in Jackson County in the mid-to-late 1980s. "We've talked to people who are good, responsible people," he said of the effort to check out Cathy's story. They confirmed her information, down to the description of the

---

[141] Jackson County Clerk of Courts, Deed Records, Marianna, Florida; Aerial Photography: Florida, Map & Image Library, George A. Smathers Libraries, University of Florida.

[142] Dale Cox, Personal Communication, January 30, 2024; Mark Davis, "30 Years on lam from Alcatraz?" *The Tampa Tribune*, January 20, 1991.

men who lived in the house. "They are not crackpots," Dennis emphasized.[143]

Federal authorities agreed with him on the reliability of the information gathered during the Jackson County investigation. Marshal McClendon later described how something kept drawing him back to the vicinity, telling reporters that he sometimes drove up and down the dirt roads of Jackson County. "I don't have anything to go on other than a gut feeling," he said. "I feel like it's possible those men were there." It was as close as any key authority actively involved in the investigation has ever come to admitting that the escape was successful and that two of the three inmates were likely near Greenwood in the 1980s.[144]

Cox wrote an article about the Greenwood claims for the *San Francisco Journal*, a Bay Area legal newspaper. "It appeared on Christmas Eve if I remember right, of that year," he said, "and Christmas and Christmas Eve is usually a slow time in the media, so newspapers all over the country picked up this story I had written about 'Anglin brothers spotted near Two Egg, Florida.'" The writer had humorously datelined his front-page story from the little crossroads of Two Egg, a beloved Florida community just east of Greenwood. In his interview with Cox for the article, Marshal McClendon elaborated that he and his deputies were "looking for two of the three escapees, the Anglin brothers, who were raised in this area, possibly escaped and came back to the area." The U.S. Marshal went on to confirm the investigation had generated leads that went beyond Cathy's story. A second woman came forward to report that she recognized the aged photograph of Clarence Anglin used in the Unsolved Mysteries broadcast. The man matching it, she said, lived on a farm near Marianna, Florida. She provided investigators with a detailed description of Anglin's height, eye color, and other characteristics, even though the image used in the broadcast was in black and white. A third informant also told investigators that the man

---

[143] *Ibid.*
[144] *Ibid.*

matching Clarence Anglin's description lived on a farm near Marianna. Greenwood is only nine miles by road from Marianna.[145]

Cox assumed that his 1990 article about the Greenwood investigation would generate significant interest. He was correct. John P. McDaniel, the retired sheriff of Jackson County, confirmed the historian's description of a strange incident immediately following the article's publication. Don DeNevi, a historian and author from California, wanted to come to Jackson County and look for the men himself. He made his first contact with Dale Cox in early 1991:

> ...I received a call from a professor who was also a writer who lived in Marin County, California, which figures into the escape from Alcatraz story because that's where Angel Island is that the inmates had told other prisoners they were going to try to reach. And he was writing a book called *Riddle of the Rock* about this, and all of a sudden, he became extremely interested in coming to see me. I didn't know what to make of it. And then he mentioned that he wanted their sister with him. I didn't have a problem with meeting their sister. I've known many members of the Anglin family through the years without even putting two and two together and even realizing they were connected to the Alcatraz escape.

Sheriff McDaniel also agreed to meet the writer and a sister of the Anglin brothers while they were in Marianna for their meeting with Cox. The situation subsequently changed, however, and although Cox did talk with the sister (her name is withheld here as a courtesy), DeNevi arrived in Marianna with a former girlfriend of John Anglin. Retired Sheriff McDaniel described what happened next:

---

[145] *San Francisco Daily Journal*, December 24, 1990.

> They came to Marianna and I met them at the Sheriff's Office. It was on a, I believe, a Saturday. And he began to interview me about it, you know, and he wanted to go to one of the relatives' houses, which would be just a little north and west of Greenwood. So I agreed and I sat there and talked to him and he talked quite a bit about the Anglin brothers and what they had gotten into and so forth.

After a lengthy conversation with Cox and McDaniel, DeNevi asked if the sheriff would accompany him to a house in northern Jackson County where other relatives of the Anglin brothers resided:

> I went with him out to the house where those people lived that were related to them. I believe they said they were cousins, and they denied seeing them in years, and this, that and the other. And he, of course, he wouldn't believe that. He believed that they had been there. I told him, I said, 'Whoa. You are not out here to accuse these people of anything. You come on and go back to the courthouse.' We went back to the courthouse, and he began to think that I was in collusion with them and good old boy politics to hide them out. And then the U.S. Marshals office got involved and I believe you [referencing Dale Cox] were involved in that.

The author from California was unaware that the U.S. Marshals Service was aware of the meeting in Marianna. He arrived as the investigation sparked by "Cathy's" revelations was still underway. Deputy marshals were surreptitiously on hand and kept the two visitors under visual and electronic surveillance for the entire day. Cox remembers it well:

109

We were all under surveillance by the U.S. Marshals Service. That's something that's never been told publicly but is an absolute fact. He was asking us all kinds of questions about the Anglin brothers and to be honest they were questions that I didn't know the answers to, and the sheriff didn't know the answers to. We answered as best we could. And he began to accuse us of withholding information from him. In fact, even accused the sheriff of being a typical Southern "small town sheriff probably allied with the Ku Klux Klan."

The Klan allegation fell flat with McDaniel. He immediately threatened to throw the writer out of his office. DeNevi calmed enough for the conversation to continue, but the California writer did not find what he was looking for. He left Jackson County convinced that Cathy's story must have been false. DeNevi spent less than six hours in the county and only around one hour in Greenwood.

The presence of a U.S. Marshals surveillance team in Marianna during the 1980s might seem incredibly long after the prison break. Still, surveillance by federal officers has been a big part of the Alcatraz escape story. Guy Anglin is a cousin of the Anglin brothers. He is also a veteran of the U.S. Marine Corps and a noted conservationist. He got a first-hand lesson in the U.S. Government's surveillance of his family when he came home from the war in Vietnam:

I was released from active duty in the Marine Corps in November of 1972. I moved back to Auburndale (Florida), and I had recently married, and we had bought a house in Auburndale. I was at work one day and the FBI showed up at the door and knocked on the door, and my wife at the time answered the door. Anyway, they wanted to question her to make sure that I wasn't Clarence or John Anglin, I guess. She didn't know anything about all of that. She had never heard of the Anglin brothers, so she sent them over to my mother. Of course, my mother was not happy at all about her sending the FBI to her house. But anyway, they went over and questioned my mother as well about me. That sort of thing has happened pretty much throughout my life.

The FBI's interactions with members of the Anglin family did not always go well. The kin of the brothers made it clear that they knew nothing about the escape and had not seen John or Clarence Anglin in years. Guy Anglin's father, for example, did not like it when an FBI agent accused him of lying:

> After we moved to Auburndale, he was in the trucking business for a number of years and then he became a mechanic for Commercial Carrier Corporation. One day, the FBI came to the job site and asked him questions about his brother. They were looking for someone and as it turned out he was working for my dad's brother, my uncle Albert Anglin. Dad told them that he didn't know the guy, so they left but they came back later and said that they found out he was off on a trip with a relief driver with my uncle. And they told him, "Well, you said that you didn't know this fellow, and he's off with your brother right now." And Dad said, "Well, you know, Albert looks after his own business, and I look after my own business." And then the FBI agent said, "Well, your name is Anglin. Are you related to the Anglins that escaped from Alcatraz?" And Daddy said, "Yeah, they're my cousins." And the FBI

agent said, "Well, I think you've been lying to me." And that wasn't the thing to say.[146]

Calling a man of any race a liar in the South, especially in the 1960s or 1970s, was akin to slapping him in the face. "He hit him," says Anglin of what his father did to the federal agent, "and knocked him right out the back door amongst the garbage cans. And the guy got up and left." To his credit, the agent took his punishment for the challenge in stride and never brought charges against the outraged man. Guy Anglin also mentions Greenwood as one of the places he heard about in family rumors, as an area where John and Clarence Anglin might have been hiding out.

What became of the escapees – if they were the escapees – after 1989, when they left the Greenwood area? Another 35 years have passed, and no trace of them has been found. The popular and usually authoritative "Find-A-Grave" website claims that Clarence Anglin died in North Dakota but points to no specific gravesite there. Another rumor holds that one of them remains behind in the city of Graceville in Jackson County, Florida, also in a grave. Once again, however, no specific gravesite can be pointed out.

While no more significant sightings of the men have been reported in 35 years, that does not mean the case has remained quiet. Over the more than three decades since his international article on the Greenwood investigation was published, Dale Cox received a series of unusual communications from a male individual that he believes was one of the Anglin brothers:

> I received contacts from someone who never said they were one of the escapees but gave a lot of information. And I later found out that someone was also writing to the San Francisco Police, claiming to be

---

[146] Anglin, Interview.

John Anglin at about the same time periods. When I compared the two, the wording was similar. They told me that only one was left alive, which is also what the Anglin letter to the San Francisco Police – alleged Anglin letter – says, that when that person is deceased, then the truth will come out.

Cox says he last spoke with the man in 2016, two years before it was revealed in 2018 that a man claiming to be John Anglin had written to the San Francisco Police Department five years earlier. In the following and final chapter, the historian reveals for the first time the story that he had promised not to tell until ten years had passed.

Chapter Eleven

The Chase Comes to an End

It was bound to end. When they left Alcatraz Island on June 11, 1962, Clarence Anglin, John Anglin, and Frank Lee Morris knew that sooner or later, they would be caught – whether by law or by time was the only question. In the end, it was time. Time is the pursuer that catches all of us, no matter how hard we run.

Many experts have offered various opinions on the three men and the measures they would need to take to escape and evade the law successfully. None of these individuals, of course, has ever eluded law enforcement for sixty years. Ultimately, evidence indicates that the Alcatraz escapees ignored most of the rules laid down for them by the experts. They also do not appear to have lived "crime-free and peaceful" lives as some have proclaimed on their behalf. They did what they had to do to survive. To the best of the authors' knowledge, they did not physically harm anyone during their years on the run; however, their actions were not without consequence. The men likely committed armed robberies and terrified innocent people, including at least one child. They were associated with drug smugglers – men and women who were in the business of destroying lives and families. By communicating with Alfred Anglin and inviting him to join them, they unintentionally contributed to his death. The loss of a brother is a heavy burden to bear. This act alone caused enormous pain for parents and family members, and likely for John and Clarence Anglin, too.

Morris and the Anglins also became legends. The Alcatraz Escape is an incredible story of three men who defied seemingly impossible odds to escape the system. Clint Eastwood brought a much taller version of Frank Morris to life, portraying him as the leader of a successful escape in a film seen by millions. Based on the evidence, Clarence Anglin could easily have been the leader of the plan instead of Morris. From a Hollywood perspective, it worked better to have the lone figure, Morris, lead the escape with the Anglin brothers as his sidekicks. The movie kicked the thriving cottage industry of Alcatraz escape books and television specials into overdrive. You will soon be able to add this one to the pile because one of those television specials led to a key breakthrough in the case.

Alcatraz: Escape to the Wiregrass differs from most books on the topic. While we set out to solve the mystery, as most authors do, our narrative is as much a history of how the 1962 escape touched a rural region of the country as it is a story of Alcatraz prison itself. What the eyewitnesses and victims of the Bank of Columbia robbery experienced in 1958, for example, has never been told in detail sufficient to explain how the crime brought about a loss of innocence for a small Alabama town. No one has explored the significant potential links between the crimes in Brundidge, Jay, and Marianna and Morris and the Anglins. Finally, this is the story of how one man, as he describes it, "stumbled into" the Alcatraz escape investigation and became fascinated by it. Dale Cox has never been obsessed with it like other writers he has met, but it has always been a curiosity. And he has one more story to tell.

In the months following the U.S. Marshals Service investigation at Greenwood, which made national news, and after a California author came to town seeking a scoop, Jackson County returned to normal. Humorous tales were told about how, when Deputy Marshals asked the postmaster in Greenwood if he recognized an intentionally aged image of Clarence Anglin, he replied, "Yes." In uncharacteristic excitement, they asked him where he had seen the man. "On Unsolved Mysteries the other night," he replied with a sly grin. Similar good-natured ribbing continued around the county for years afterward. Today, people not directly connected to the original investigation often provide factually incorrect versions, as if they were central to it. This is not unique to small communities.

Dale Cox's days as a reporter ended shortly after he stumbled into the real Alcatraz investigation. Being a television reporter was never his chosen profession, and he did not particularly enjoy it. He says today that he was good at the job because he disliked it so much and wanted only to work his way up and out of it as quickly as possible. He left WJHG in 1992 to pursue a career in broadcast management. Shortly before then, however, he heard from an unidentified man who claimed to have read Cox's story about Clarence Anglin and Frank Lee Morris possibly being in Greenwood, Florida. Here is the story of their communications as related verbally by Dale Cox in 2024:

> The first time I heard from this individual was in December of 1991. Fortunately, we made contact because I already knew, although I had not announced it, that I would be leaving soon for a new position with a station in Indiana. He mentioned that he read the article about the search for the Alcatraz escapees in Greenwood and found it fascinating. He said it was amazing how a cousin, Cathy, would turn on a family member for money, but that was the kind of world we lived in, and that family mattered more than anything. He also said it was interesting to read about how hard the government was still trying to catch "them boys." That was it, but something about it gave me one of those "weird" feelings you get occasionally.[147]

---

[147] Dale Cox, Interview with author, September 30, 2024.

Cox believes the contact was from either one of the Anglin brothers or a family member close to them. According to a timeline kept by the historian, the individual's next contact came nearly six months later, in April 1992. The number from which he called had a California area code. He asked more about the investigation at Greenwood, but Cox had no updates to give him. When the conversation turned to Cathy's claims of seeing the escapees while visiting nearby relatives, the man unexpectedly offered the names of the woman's family members. Their surname was not then and has not since been made public:

> That perked up my ears when he casually mentioned their names. Cathy's family name was closely guarded and had not appeared in my story published in the San Francisco Journal or any other media reports I had seen. He knew it, though, and by disclosing it, he revealed to me that he knew more about the story than he was letting on. That "weird" feeling I had from his first contact came back and was multiplied by 10.[148]

The contact between the two men continued irregularly over the next several years. Each time, the caller would drop a name or tidbit of information that was not public. On one occasion, they discussed the Alcatraz escape. Cox mentioned that he had recently seen a television show featuring an athletic event where people swam from Alcatraz Island to the mainland. The man jokingly asked how they did it without being "eaten by sharks" and then volunteered that he had been in the water of San Francisco Bay himself. He said it was cold but that people who claimed it was too cold to swim in were "crazy or liars." The historian cautiously asked what it was like to swim in the bay, and the contact told him that he "wouldn't want to swim in it when it is all choppy and breezy" but that sometimes, at night, it was "smooth as silk."

---

[148] *Ibid.*

He also said it took him a "bit to warm up" after his swim, but that "you could probably do it yourself."[149]

The string of phone calls gradually faded away. Was the caller one of the escapees? One of their family members? Was he a law enforcement source with inside access to non-public information about the escape? Then came a blog comment posted in 2014, after Cox released a new article on the Greenwood story:

> Nice post. One of these men is still alive, both have lived full, good lives that did not include a return by either of them to a life of crime, and have raised wonderful families. There are a few details you conveniently left out of your story that reveals more about them on a personal note and circumstances that landed them in Alcatraz. The conditions they experienced were horrible, and when given a choice, they took a chance as opposed to suffering. Neither ever made excuses for what they did but they have lived good Christian lives and done a lot of good in the world since escaping.
>
> When both have passed on there are arrangements to tell there [*sic.*] story for the benefit of others.[150]

Cox is uncertain whether the comment was from one of the escapees or someone with intimate knowledge of them. He notes that it contains some of the same spelling errors as known writing samples of John and Clarence Anglin, but has reached no conclusions about who could have written it.

---

[149] *Ibid.*

[150] "Informant claims one of Alcatraz escapees is still alive," https://twoegg.blogspot.com/2014/06/informant-claims-one-of-alcatraz.html, retrieved September 1, 2024.

The legend of the Anglin brothers and Frank Morris, their daring escape from Alcatraz, and the decades of speculation that followed took a startling turn in early 2024. The whispers, the theories, the hopeful glimpses were overshadowed by a quiet, yet definitive, revelation: John William Anglin was dead. The last of the three escapees to remain alive and at large, he died of age and illness in the northwestern United States. He was 94 years old, having lived free for 61 years after escaping United States Penitentiary, Alcatraz Island. He outlived his brother, Clarence, and their friend, Frank Lee Morris, by decades. The location of his death adds credence to a letter received by the San Francisco Police Department in 2013. The writer of that document claimed to be John Anglin:

> My name is John Anglin. I escape from Alcatraz in June 1962 with my brother Clarence and Frank Morris. I am 83 years old and in bad shape. I have cancer. Yes we all made it that night but barely!
>
> Frank passed away in October 2008. His grave is in Alexandria under a nother name. My brother died in 2011.
>
> If you announce on T.V. that I will be promised to go to jail for no more than a year and get medical attention I will write you back to let you know exactly where I am. This is no joke. This is for real....

The writer went on to state that he lived in North Dakota for many years, ending in 2003, but it "was too Dam Cold." He reported that he lived in Seattle "for most of my years after the escape." He concluded by telling the police department that he was "in Southern California now." Still, he did not clarify whether that meant he was living in the region or visiting while he waited for an answer to his surrender offer. If the latter was the case, then he waited for an announcement that never came. The San Francisco Police Department did not take the handwritten document seriously, and another five years passed before KPIX-TV discovered its existence. The television station released the letter to the world in 2018.

The U.S. Marshals Service turned the document over to the FBI for handwriting analysis. The results were "inconclusive," and marshals announced that they considered the incident closed.[151]

The claims included in the letter give it a thread of authenticity. It suggests that John spent most of his life apart from Clarence and Frank. This is consistent with the claims made by Cathy in the 1980s, following the *Unsolved Mysteries* episode. She told marshals that Clarence and Frank were living near Greenwood, but made no mention of seeing John during her visits. The letter writer's statement that Frank died in 2008 and was buried under an assumed name in Alexandria also offers a thread that may lead to the truth. Which Alexandria did he mean? The best-known American cities with this name are in Virginia and Louisiana. Frank Lee Morris had connections to both. He lived in Louisiana for many years, and his police records indicate familiarity with Alexandria, a city located near the center of the state. His record also shows strong connections to the District of Columbia, of which the Alexandria in Virginia was a part until March 1847. His mother lived in Washington, D.C., and he spent time in reform school there. The writer gave death dates for both Frank and Clarence that fit the timeline of the alleged sightings in Greenwood, Florida.

Curiously, the letter's claim that Frank Morris died first in October 2008, with Clarence Anglin living another three years, is consistent with alleged sightings of a man named Carl Miller living in Alabama. Carl Miller was one of the known aliases used by Clarence Anglin. Claims of a suspicious man using this name first surfaced in 1962-1963. While FBI agents investigated the reports and ruled out a connection to the escapee, they never actually talked to the individual. Nor do agents' reports indicate they were aware of how extensively Clarence used the alias during the years before he was sentenced to federal prison. Then, in the years after the alleged Greenwood sightings, the mysterious Carl Miller

---

[151] "Letter Originally Written By 1962 Alcatraz Island Escapee Surfaces," CBS News Bay Area (KPIX), January 22, 2018, https://www.cbsnews.com/sanfrancisco/news/letter-allegedly-written-alcatraz-island-escapee-surfaces/ retrieved July 22, 2024.

resurfaced in Alabama. Law enforcement sources indicate that eyewitnesses viewed photographs of Clarence Anglin that had been adapted to reflect his possible appearance as an older man. Several responded that the individual in these images was known to them not as Clarence Anglin, but Carl Miller. Sightings of this man continued in Alabama until the winter of 2010-2011. No eyewitness has reported seeing the man since that time. This sudden end to alleged sightings is consistent with the San Francisco letter writer's claim that Clarence died in 2011.

In 2024, eleven years after the letter was written, historian Dale Cox received contact from a long-trusted source with news that John Anglin was dead. The source was a family member of the Anglin brothers, but one who has never been named in any of the reporting about the escape. Their name does appear in the police record that the two brothers compiled in the years leading up to the robbery of the Bank of Columbia. Within months of Cox learning from his source that John had died, law enforcement officers in the region were given the same information by other family members of the escapees. As was the case with the historian's source, those who spoke privately with law enforcement agencies reported that John died at an undisclosed location in the northern Great Plains region. They requested anonymity.

The confirmation of John's death was neither a sudden nor unexpected disclosure. It was the culmination of decades-long, clandestine connections between "off the radar" family members and the escapee. John Anglin, operating under an assumed identity, maintained contact with distant relatives in the Southeast for many years, especially after the deaths of Frank Morris and Clarence. This communication, carefully orchestrated and shrouded in secrecy, provided a lifeline to his past while allowing him to live a life hidden from the U.S. Marshals Service.

This revelation raises several crucial points. For years, the possibility of the Anglin brothers' survival was a matter of speculation. The confirmation of John's death, however, establishes that at least one of

122

them survived the escape and lived for decades afterward. The fact that the escapee maintained contact with relatives who did not seek publicity for such a long period indicates a well-established network of secrecy. This network, involving family members and friends, allowed him to live undetected. That John died in the upper Great Plains establishes a significant geographical link. This region, previously not a focal point, has now become a crucial area of interest. While the news confirms John's fate, it leaves the mystery of Clarence Anglin unresolved. The question of exactly when and where he died remains open, although he may have been living in Alabama under the name of Carl Miller at the time.

The confirmation brings a sense of closure to the long-standing mystery. It also marks the end of an era, as John Anglin was a symbol and living link to the daring and enduring mystery. Several factors likely contributed to John's living apart from Frank Morris and Clarence Anglin. Even within a close-knit group, individuals have different personalities and goals. After a high-stress event, such as an escape, these differences may become more pronounced. The three men likely had different ideas of how to live their lives as fugitives. Remaining together as a group of three increased their risk of detection. Separating was a strategic decision aimed at improving their chances of long-term survival. It is much harder to track down three people on separate paths than to track down one group. Living separately also allowed each person to create their identity and live quietly without drawing attention.

The Anglin brothers had strong family ties, but John Anglin chose to live apart from close relatives in his attempt to evade capture. While he maintained contact with certain relatives, they were not immediate family members. This is a clue as to how the escapee could contact his brothers, Robert Anglin and Alfred Anglin, without attracting attention from the FBI or U.S. Marshals Service. These agencies monitored the phone calls and mail of the parents, siblings, close relatives, and friends of the escapees. No direct contact between individuals believed to be the escapees and these friends and relatives ever took place – at least according to law enforcement. Yet somehow, both Alfred Anglin and

Robert Anglin received information on the success of the escape and the whereabouts of their brothers. Since modern electronic communication did not exist in 1962, and would have been monitored anyway, the only way the escapees could have contacted these two trusted family members was through intermediaries known to be trustworthy. In other words, family members with strong connections to the escapees who remained away from the publicity surrounding them. This description fits the Anglin family sources who spoke with both historian Cox and local law enforcement in the Southeast.

The FBI laboratory's examinations of the 2013 San Francisco letter focused on handwriting comparisons, fingerprint analysis, and DNA testing. None of these examinations returned conclusive results. This means the forensic analysts could neither confirm nor deny that John Anglin wrote the letter. The inability of forensic analysts to *disprove* that John Anglin wrote the letter to the San Francisco Police Department means precisely that: they could not rule him out as the author. It's crucial to understand the nuances of this. Scientists were unable to verify the authenticity of the letter. "Inconclusive" is not the same as "confirmed." The lack of evidence to say "he didn't write it" is essential, but is not the same as having evidence to say "he did write it." The inconclusive results suggest that John Anglin may have written the letter, but it was impossible to obtain a positive handwriting match. It remains a possibility, albeit one without firm supporting evidence.

Analysis of the letter highlights the limitations of forensic science. Factors like the age of a document, the quality of the sample, or the absence of a known sample for comparison can limit the effectiveness of forensic tests. The letter is written in cursive, while many of the confirmed handwriting samples of John and Clarence Anglin were done in print. The writer also stated that he was in poor health, battling cancer. Age and health affects handwriting, contributing to the difficulty analysts face when comparing documents to much older samples.

The inconclusive results contribute to the ongoing ambiguity surrounding the Anglin brothers' escape and its aftermath. The alleged letter. the Greenwood sightings, and the information provided by family sources present a scenario in which John Anglin lived independently, while Clarence Anglin and potentially Frank Morris were together. This consistency, while not proving the letter's authenticity, does provide a point of alignment between three separate sources of information.

So, what impact does the confirmation that John Anglin died in 2024 and the admission that Fred Brizzi never claimed the two men in his photograph were Clarence and John have on claims that the escapees lived out their lives in Brazil? The revelation that Brizzi never explicitly identified the purported Brazil photograph as depicting the Anglin brothers significantly alters the narrative surrounding the escape. This removes a crucial piece of alleged direct evidence linking the brothers to Brazil. Previously, the photo, presented by the Anglin family, was considered a potential visual confirmation of their survival and relocation. It still might be, but the evidentiary chain is broken. Since Brizzi never said the photograph was of the Anglin brothers, assuming it to be so means attempting to read the man's reasons for including it in the packet of material he gave to their family. His ex-wife, as has been noted, remembered the photograph, but told reporters that Brizzi never mentioned the Anglins. The two men shown were in the image simply to provide scale to the giant ant mound that is its central feature. Brizzi kept this photograph for years before giving it to the Anglin family. It is reasonable to question why he did that if the image was supposed to offer proof of life for relatives.

With claims about Brizzi thrown into the air, the photo's significance is diminished, and it no longer serves as anything other than a photograph of two men who resemble John and Clarence Anglin. This shift highlights the importance of verifying evidence and claims, especially in cold cases where speculation and hearsay can easily obscure the facts. It reinforces that the investigation into the Anglin brothers' fate must rely on verifiable evidence, not just assumptions or interpretations. Did analysts rule the photograph as likely authentic? Yes and no. Analysts consulted by some family members and associated writers gave the image considerable merit. Federal government laboratories, however, deemed it inconclusive. Which determination is correct?

The differing conclusions highlight the subjective nature of photo analysis and the varying standards of evidence. The family's analyst, presumably hired by the Anglin relatives or cooperating writers, focused on visual comparisons, facial recognition, and potentially other forensic techniques. Their conclusion that the photo was likely authentic relies heavily on claims that it was supposed to represent the Anglin brothers. Had these analysts known that the long-time holder of the image never made that claim, would their opinions have changed? The analysts consulted by the Marshals Service, as law enforcement professionals, adhere to stricter standards of evidence. Their "inconclusive" determination means they could neither confirm nor deny the identities of the two men. This was due to factors including poor image quality, insufficient points of comparison, the passage of time, which can alter facial features, and the need for absolute certainty in legal matters. Again, the question must be asked: Would knowledge that the longtime holder of the photograph never claimed it was the Anglins have changed their conclusion?

This entire episode highlights the questions that often arise when potential pieces of evidence become the subject of a media frenzy without all the essential facts being considered. What might be convincing to a family seeking closure may not meet the rigorous standards of a law enforcement investigation. The media, unfortunately, is often eager to publicize such evidence without conducting a thorough background investigation.

The suggested timeline of deaths – Frank Morris in 2008, Clarence Anglin in 2011, and John Anglin in 2024 – holds significant implications for the narrative of the Alcatraz escape. This sequence suggests a gradual unraveling of the escapees' clandestine lives over decades. It indicates that they successfully evaded capture for a considerable period, with Frank Morris potentially being the first to succumb to age or illness. He was the oldest of the three. Clarence Anglin's death, a few years later, further diminished the group, leaving John Anglin to live on for another decade. Finally, John's death in 2024 provided a conclusion to a mystery that has captivated the public for generations. This timeline, if ultimately verified by the disclosure of their burial places, would not only confirm their survival but also offer a glimpse into the challenges of living as fugitives for such an extended period.

The enduring mystery of the escape from Alcatraz remains a source of fascination and perplexity. From the disputed authenticity of photographs to the conflicting reports of post-escape lives, the narrative remains shrouded in uncertainty. While the reported death of John Anglin in 2024 offers a potential endpoint, it also underscores the enduring nature of the questions that persist. The convergence of details from the alleged letter, the Greenwood sightings, and the reported timeline of deaths creates a complex tapestry of possibilities, yet definitive proof remains elusive. Whether the escapees lived out their lives in quiet anonymity or succumbed to the challenges of fugitive existence, the story of Morris and the Anglin Brothers stands as a testament to the enduring power of speculation and the allure of the unknown.

The Alcatraz escape, particularly the alleged success of the Anglin brothers and Frank Morris, holds a significant place in American history for several reasons. It was an audacious challenge to authority, particularly against a prison designed to be inescapable. This resonates with the American spirit of rebellion and individual freedom. The enduring mystery has fueled decades of speculation, creating a captivating legend that has permeated popular culture through films, books, and documentaries. The escape raises profound questions about human motivation, resilience, and the desire for freedom. It is a cultural touchstone, reflecting anxieties and fascinations with crime, punishment, and the limits of control. That the case remains officially unsolved adds to the intrigue and keeps the story alive in the public mind.

The Alcatraz escape transcends a simple prison break; it has become a symbol of human ingenuity and the enduring pursuit of freedom, leaving an indelible mark on American history and popular culture.

Alcatraz: Escape to the Wiregrass

Photographs

Figure 1. The Anglin Brothers were born in Donalsonville, the county seat of Seminole County, Georgia.

Figure 2. The "boys" spent their earliest years in a rural community across the Miller County line just north of Donalsonville.

Figure 3 Columbia is a historic community in Southeast Alabama. The Anglin Brothers had family and friends there.

Figure 4 The Anglin brothers targeted Bank of Columbia (visible at left) for a daring daylight robbery. The surveilled the bank from a bench across the street.

Figure 5 The Anglin Brothers stormed the bank on a sleepy Friday morning. The three employees were threatened with handguns.

Figure 6. Historian Dale Cox examines the vault door in the Bank of Columbia with fellow historian David Hunter. The original nerve gas system is still in place, but was not triggered during the robbery since an employee opened the vault.

Figure 7. The three brothers sped away from the front of the bank. The getaway car took a sharp turn to the right at the intersection visible in the distance.

Figure 8. The escape route led east from the central intersection on the road to the Chattahoochee River and Southwest Georgia.

Photographs

Figure 9. The fleeing bank robbers headed down the hill from Columbia to the bridge over the Chattahoochee River. On the opposite side were their old stomping grounds.

Figure 10. The Chattahoochee River divides Alabama from Georgia at Columbia. The view has not changed much since the Anglin Brothers crossed after the 1958 robbery.

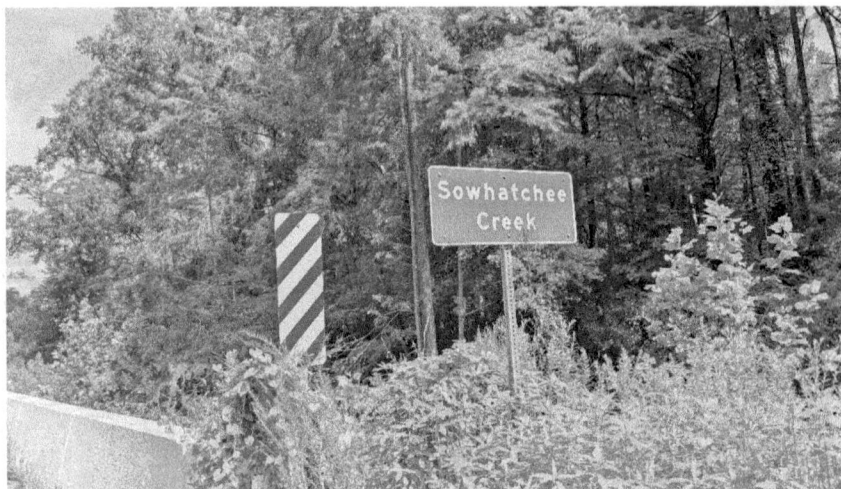

Figure 11. Sowhatchee Creek flows through woods and farmland in Southwest Georgia. The Anglin Brothers hid out here in the hours before the bank robbery.

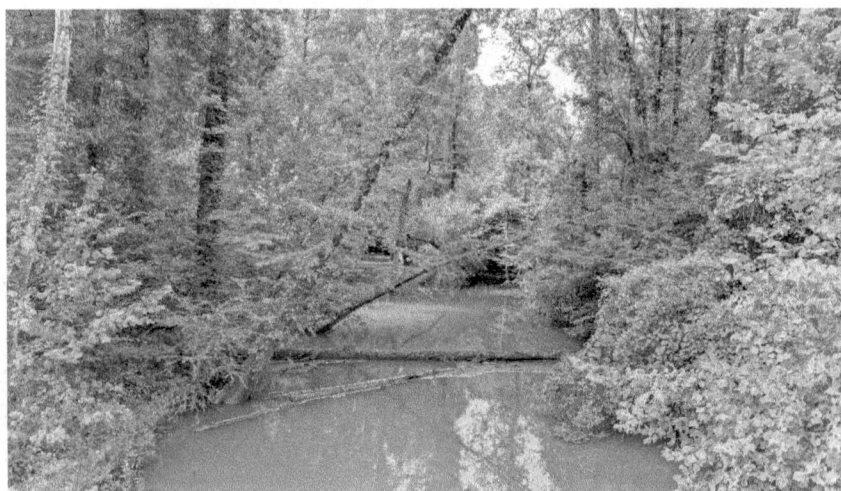

Figure 12. The creek was a popular swimming hole for the Anglins during their boyhood years. Their use of Sowhatchee as a hideout demonstrates their knowledge of the area in and around Columbia, Alabama.

136

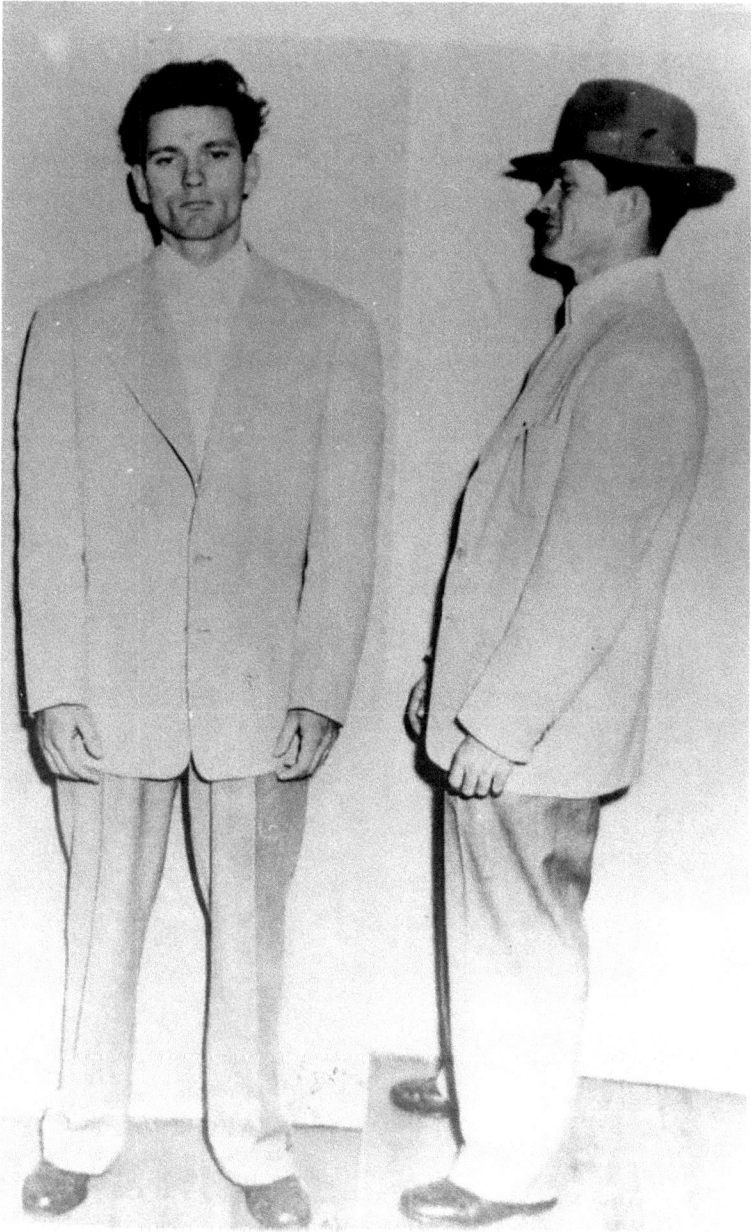

Figure 13. Frank Lee Morris was straight from the streets of New Orleans and still in his suit when he was arrested for bank burglary. (FBI)

Alfred Anglin Electrocuted
Trying To Flee From Kilby

By CHARLES CATES

One of the notorious Anglin brothers was killed Saturday night as he attempted a daring escape from Kilby prison.

Alfred Ray Anglin, 34, a convicted bank robber—whose two brothers escaped Alcatraz in 1962 and have not been heard from since—died when he was electrocuted.

"Anglin cut the bars on a second floor laundry room window with a hacksaw," prison commissioner Frank Lee said. "He had placed a rubber inner tube around the wire, but it wasn't enough protection."

A second prisoner, Althea Senn, about 40, was involved in the prison break attempt, Lee said. "It was just lucky he didn't go out the window first."

The two Anglin brothers who escaped from Alcatraz were Clarence and John. A third man, Frank Lee Morris, was with them. Authorities have been unable to find any trace of the trio.

Alfred was sentenced to prison from Houston County for his part in robbing the Columbia, Ala., bank in January, 1958. He was placed in Kilby Sept. 9, 1963, to begin serving his state and federal sentences concurrently, Lee said.

The Florida native had made four prison breaks as had his brother Clarence. The Columbia robbery netted the Anglin brothers $19,000, but federal agents caught them a few days later in Cincinnati and recovered $13,648.33 in cash and $5,000 in travelers' checks of the bank loot.

ALFRED ANGLIN
Dies In Escape Try

Figure 14. Alfred Anglin, as shown in the Montgomery Advertiser, six years after the Bank of Columbia robbery.

Figure 15. Clarence Anglin as he appeared in a mugshot taken shortly after the Bank of Columbia robbery.(FBI)

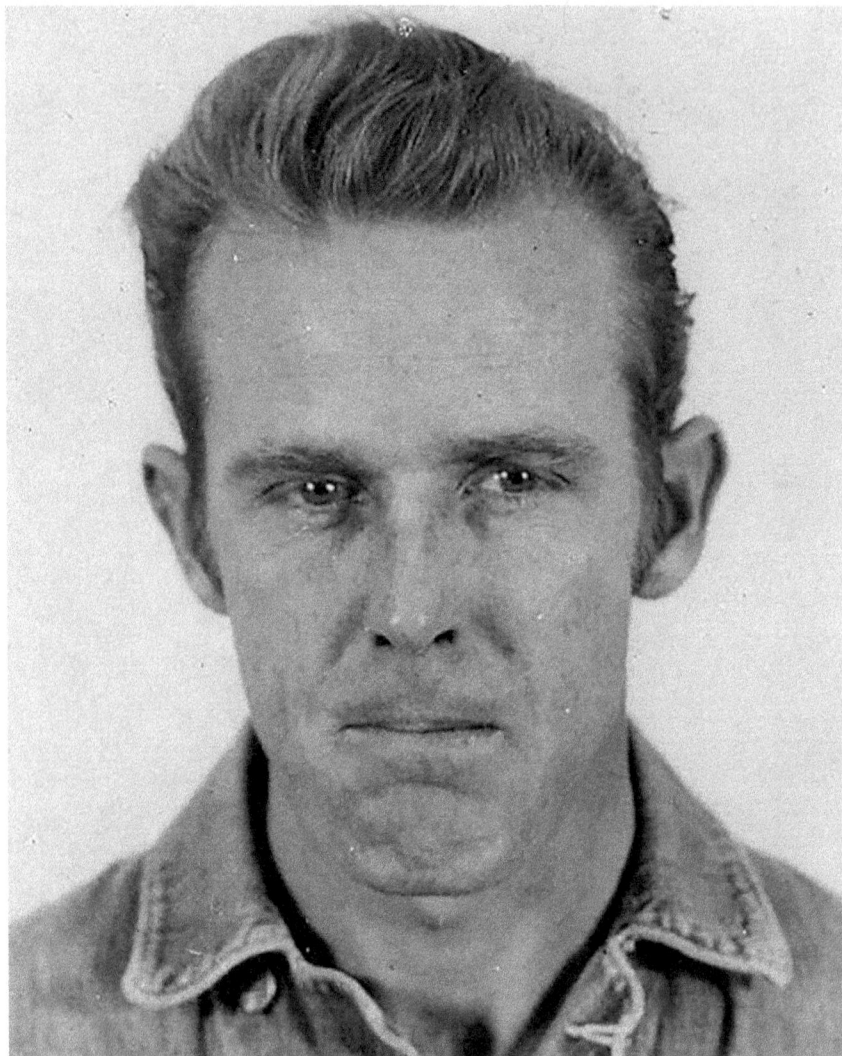

Figure 16. John Anglin's mugshot from the files of the FBI.

Figure 17. The historic Houston County Jail structure in downtown Dothan, Alabama (now used for other purposes). The Anglin Brothers were housed here during their trial.

"The Rock", Alcatraz Island, San Francisco Bay, Calif.

(C) Gabriel Moulin

Figure 18. "The Rock," as shown in a postcard, not long after the escape of Frank Morris, Clarence Anglin, and John Anglin. (NPS)

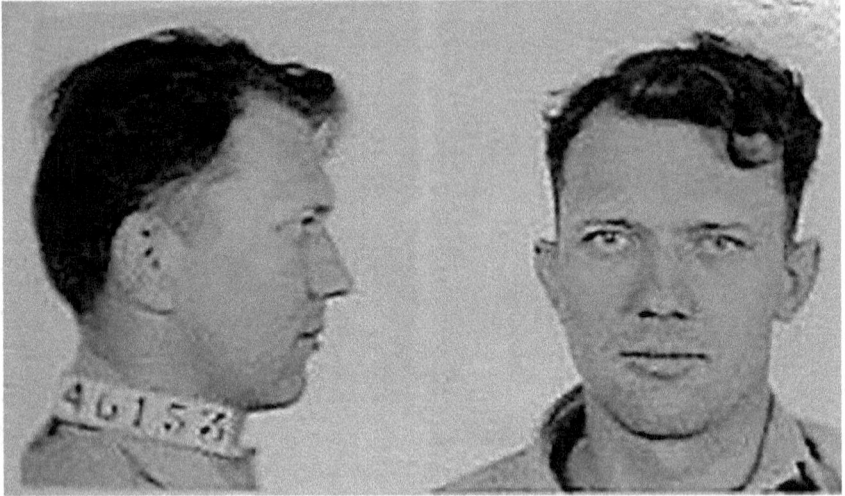

Figure 19. Ralph Roe, one of the two Oklahoma outlaws who disappeared from Alcatraz in the 1940s. (FBI)

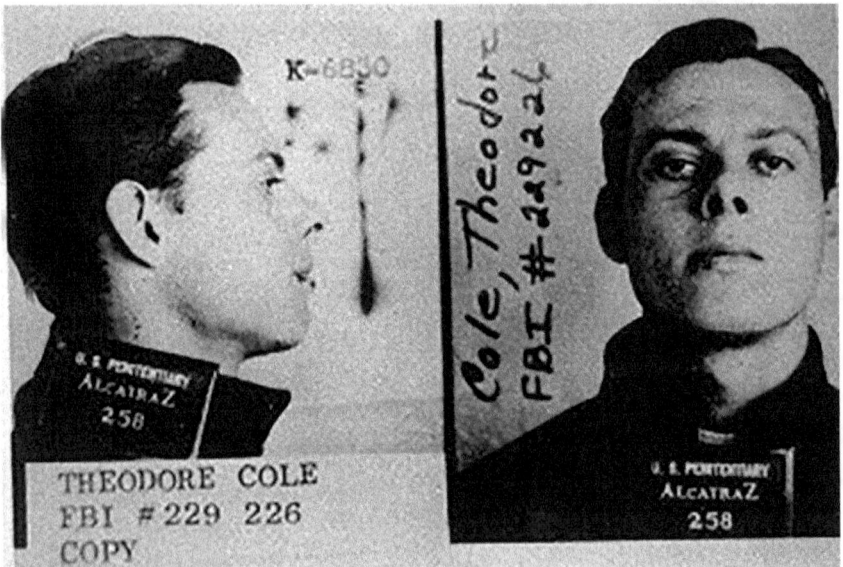

Figure 20. Theodore "Ted" Cole was the second of two Oklahoma outlaws who escaped Alcatraz in the 1940s. No trace of either man was ever found. (FBI)

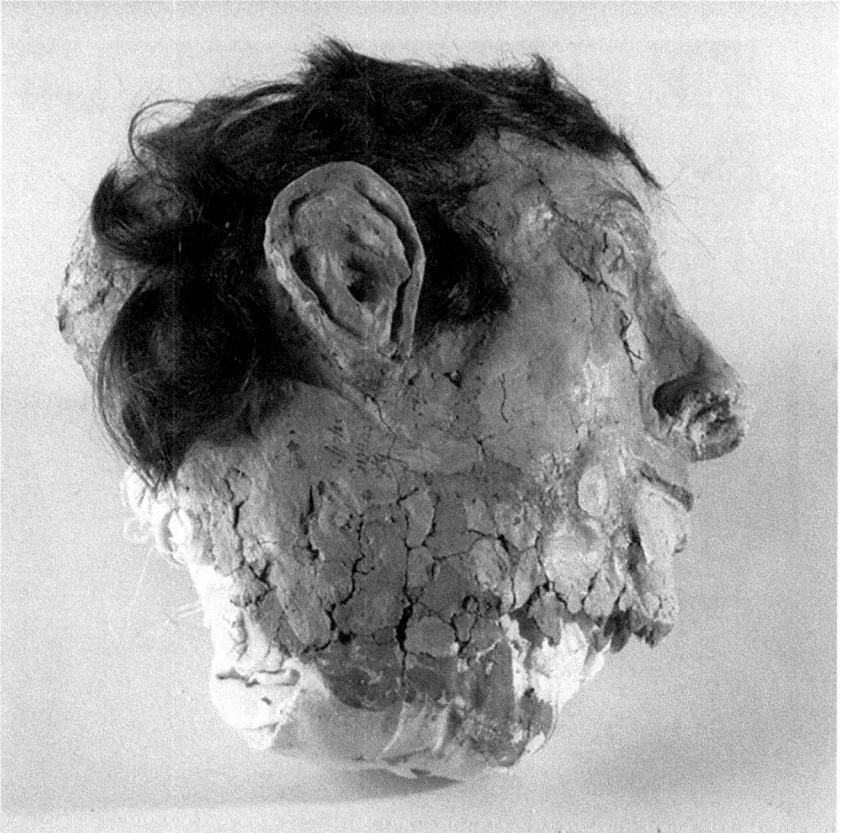

Figure 21. The handmade "dummy head" that Frank Lee Morris used to trick guards at Alcatraz on the night of the 1962 escape. (FBI)

Figure 22. A guard examines one of the cell ventilation holes through which the Anglins and Morris escaped in June 1962. (FBI)

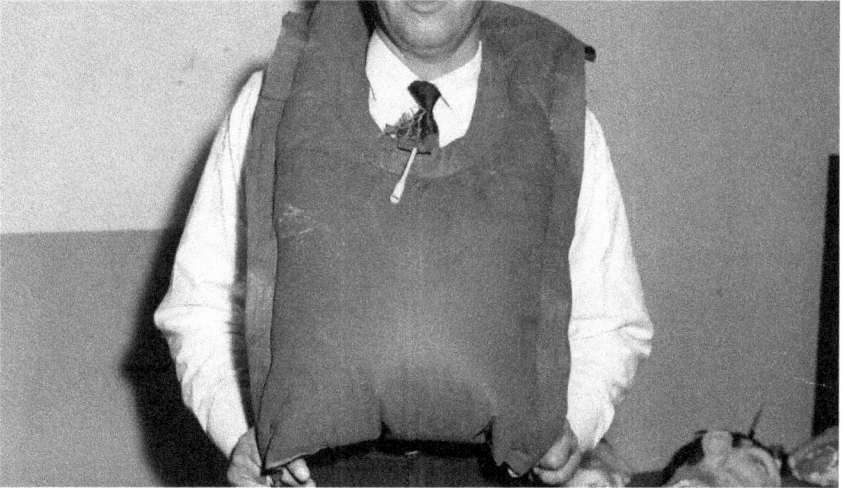

Figure 23. One of the life preservers fabricated by the escapees in 1962. FBI analysts determined they were extremely well-made. (FBI)

Figure 24. This photograph shows the route taken by the Anglins and Morris on their way from the cellhouse to San Francisco Bay. (FBI)

LIFE JACKET FOUND —NEW ESCAPE CLUE?

A home-made life jacket, similar to those made by three convicts who escaped from Alcatraz Prison on June 11, was reported to have been found in San Francisco Bay.

It was another possible clue among the many "clues," which have as yet failed to establish whether or not the three escapers are dead or alive.

A report published in San Francisco said the jacket was blood stained and matted with hair. The jacket, according to the report, was found a week ago, but no official source would say exactly where it was found or by whom.

Since the disappearance of the convicts, pieces of a wooden raft and a plastic sheeting tied in knots to provide air pockets floated up in Marin.

The report of the blood-stained jacket gave substance to the speculation of a top federal prison official that Clarence Anglin and his brother John killed the mastermind of the daring escape, Frank Morris.

Hair was matted on the life jacket, and it was still laced, indicating the wearer slipped or was pushed out of it after being slugged, according to the report.

Fred Wilkinson, deputy director of U.S. prisons, some time ago expressed a theory that the mastermind, Morris, Louisiana bank robber, might have been slain by the Anglin brothers, Alabama robbers. If their makeshift raft had become overloaded, the Anglins would probably dispose of Morris, the prison official theorized.

Figure 25. This article from Marin County's Daily Independent Journal appeared on July 5, 1962. It was one of a series of such reports carried by the paper, all conveying information about clues to a successful escape.

146

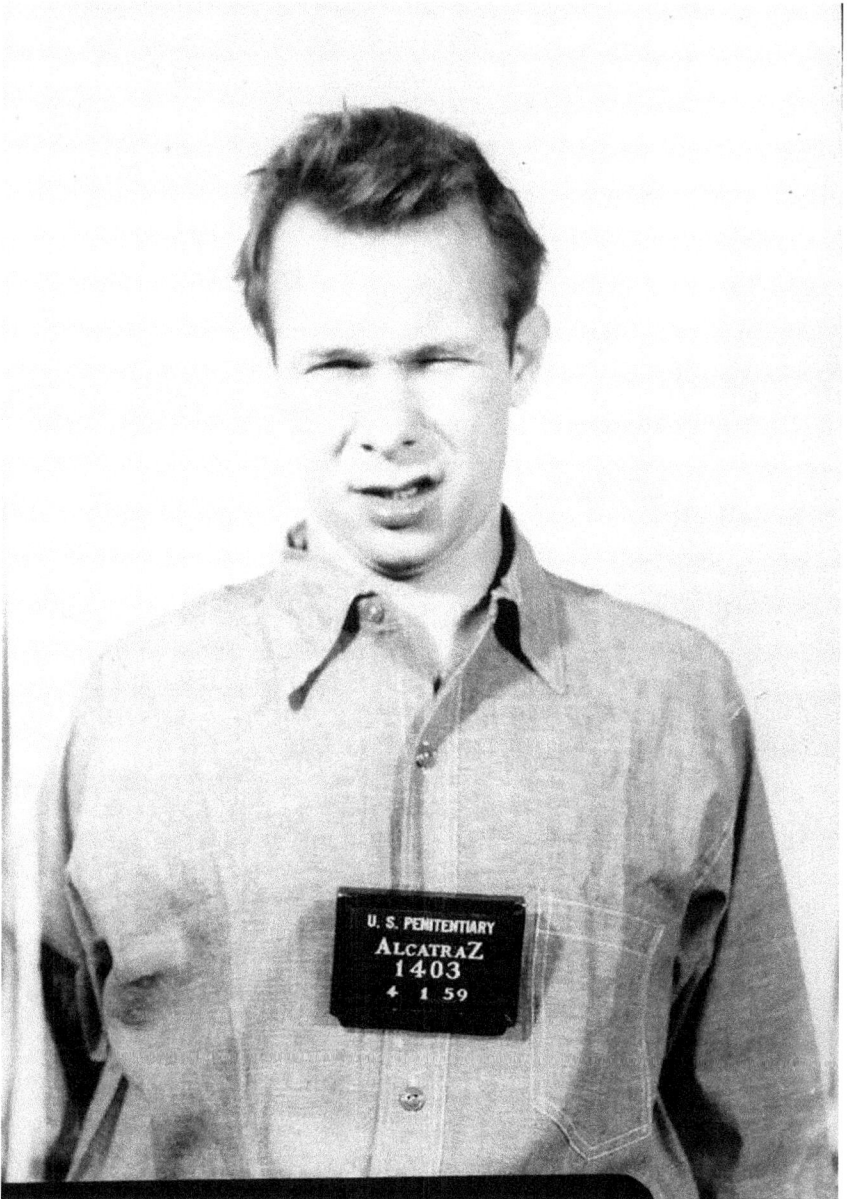

Figure 26. John Paul Scott, who escaped Alcatraz in December 1962. He swam across San Francisco Bay and crawled out of the water near the base of the Golden Gate Bridge, proving that Morris and the Anglins likely made it. (FBI)

147

PAGE TWO.......*76-1991* PH

FOR INFO DALLAS, RE SF TEL ADVISED WARDEN OLIN G. BLACKWELL,
FORTYSEVEN S. PENITENTIARY, ALCATRAZ, CALIF., ADVISED JULY TWENTYSEVEN
INSTANT THAT INMATE ███████████████████████████████████
█████████, HAD JULY TWENTY SEVEN ADVISED ASSOCIATE ARTHUR DOLLISON OF
THE FOLLOWING INFORMATION.

█████████ ADVISED THAT QUOTE ██████████ UNQUOTE, A CUSTODIAL OFFICER
FOR ALCATRAZ ON NIGHT DUTY DURING THE MONTHS OF FEB., MARCH, AND APRIL
SIXTY TWO, ALLEGEDLY RECEIVED OR WAS TO RECEIVED FIVE HUNDRED DOLLARS
FROM SUBJ FRANK LEE MORRIS ASSIST SUBJS IN ESCAPE FROM ALCATRAZ.

█████████ STATED THAT QUOTE ██████████ UNQUOTE WHO IS BELIEVED TO BE
ALCATRAZ CUSTODIAL OFFICER █████████████ EMPLOYEE OF SEVERAL
YRS., WAS TO RECEIVE ADDITIONAL TWO HUNDRED DOLLARS FROM SUBJ MORRIS
FOLLOWING ESCAPE AND AFTER ██████ HAD ARRANGED TO OBTAIN CAR FOR USE
OF ESCAPEES AFTER THEY REACHED MAINLAND.

█████████ ADVISED THAT ██████ WAS TO ARRANGE THRU ONE ████████████
A FRIEND OF JOHN ANGLIN AND FORMER INMATE LEWISBURG PEN., LEWISBURG,
PA., APPARENTLY WHILE JOHN ANGLIN WAS ALSO INMATE AT LEWISBURG, TO SECUR
CAR IN ORDER TO EFFECT THEIR ESCAPE.

END PAGE TWO.......

Figure 27. This report from the FBI file on the Alcatraz Escape details claims that guards at "the Rock" were bribed prior to the escape. The investigation revealed irregularities. (FBI)

148

Figure 28. This photograph was taken during a discussion about the Alcatraz escape. Pictured are historian Dale Cox (right), Citizens State Bank robbery eyewitness Robert Earl Standland (center), and archivist for Jackson County, Florida, Sue Tindel (left).

Figure 29. A 1963 article from the Dothan Eagle raised questions about possible involvement by the escapees in the robbery of Citizens State Bank in Marianna, Florida. (Columbia Historical Society of Alabama)

could not identify photographs of the Subject
in this case and both insisted that no individual matching
the description of ░░░░░░░░░░░░ or FRANK LEE
MORRIS had ever contacted ░░░░ at their residence.

- 79 -

Figure 30. A page from the FBI file on the Alcatraz Escape, showing the degree to which the Bureau has redacted information about the escapees provided by an inmate at the Houston County Jail in Dothan, Alabama.

150

Figure 31. A former prison friend claimed he was visited by Frank Morris at Cobb Memorial Hospital in Phenix City, Alabama. (ADAH

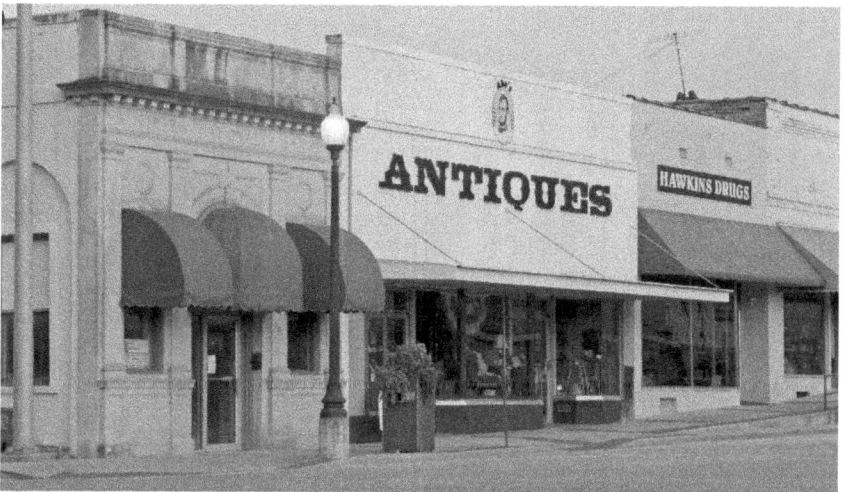

Figure 32. The First National Bank in Brundidge (left side) became a center for investigation after a local merchant accepted a fraudulent check passed by a man clerks identified as John Anglin.

Figure 33. This view of Kilby Prison near Montgomery shows the scene where Alfred Anglin died. He started climbing from one of the windows of the large structure, planning to drop down to the roof of the office building visible at left.

Figure 34. The U.S. Marshals Service descended on the community of Greenwood, Florida, after receiving information that two of the escapees were living in the vicinity.

Figure 35. Greenwood is located west of Tallahassee in Northwest Florida. It is less than a one-hour drive from Dothan, the Alabama city where the Anglin Brothers were convicted.

Figure 36. A relative claimed that two of the escapees were living on a Northwest Florida peanut farm in the 1980s. Peanut harvesting is underway near Greenwood in this photo.

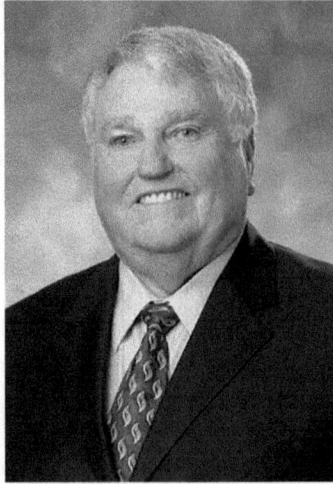

Figure 37. U.S. Marshal Mac McLendon continued to drive dirt roads in the Greenwood area for years after the reported sighting there. (U.S. Marshals Service)

Figure 38. Did Clarence Anglin and Frank Morris escape Alcatraz to live part of their lives on a farm near Greenwood, Florida? This photo shows peanuts on the vine after they have been dug for harvesting.

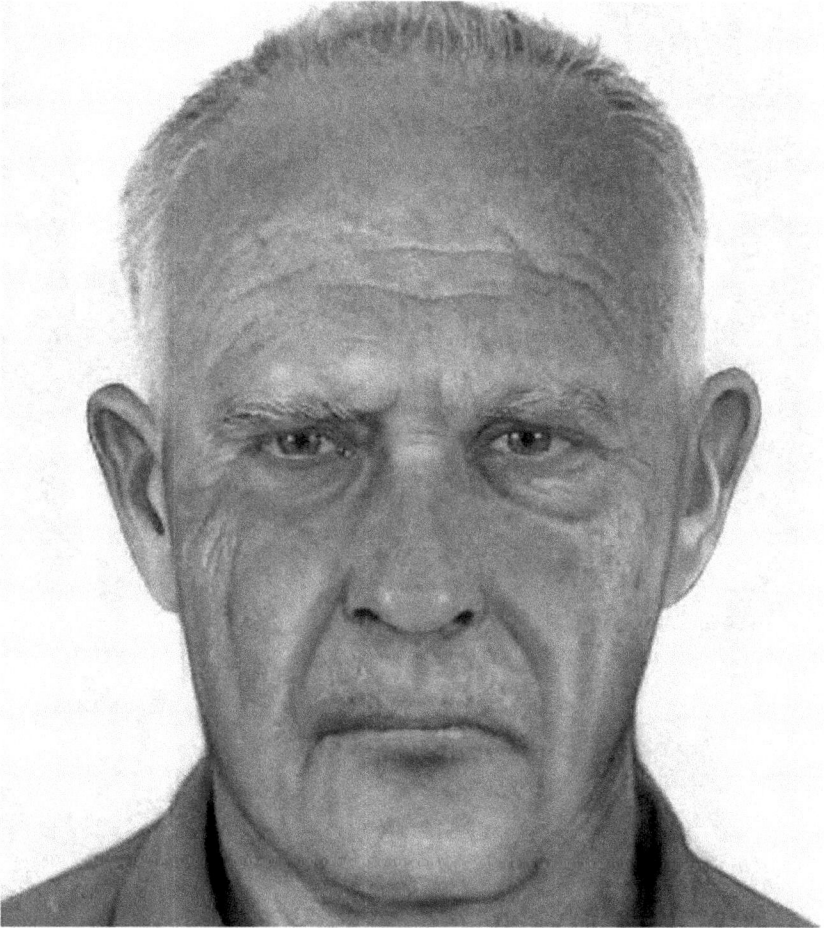

Figure 39. An intentionally-aged image of Clarence Anglin shared by the U.S. Marshals Service to show his possible appearance. (U.S. Marshals Service)

Figure 40. Frank Morris, shown here in an intentionally-aged image, was reportedly the first of the three escapees to die. (U.S. Marshals Service)

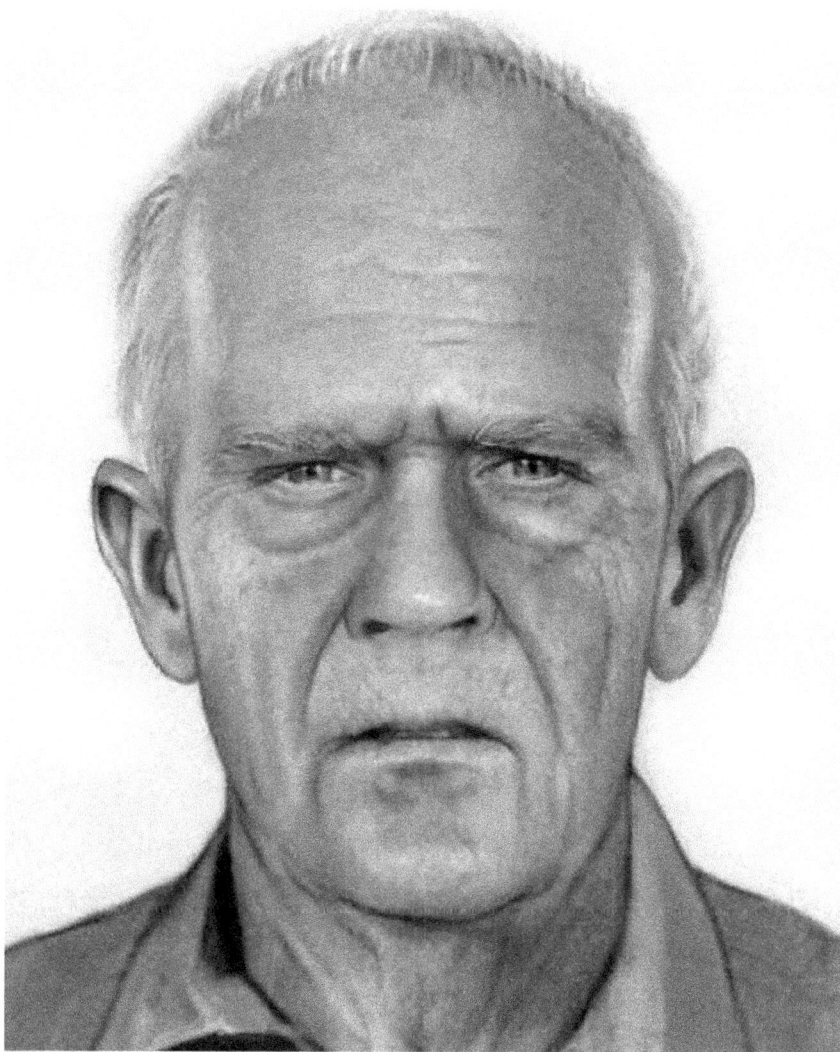

Figure 41. Did John Anglin look similar to this when sources claim he died as this book was being prepared for publication? (U.S. Marshals Service)

References

Documents

University of Florida. George A. Smathers Libraries. Map & Image Library. Aerial Photography: Florida. Accessed October 26, 2023. http://ufdc.ufl.edu/aerialphotos.

Federal Bureau of Investigation. Theodore Cole and Ralph Roe Escape File. 1937–1938. FBI Records. Washington, D.C.

C. A. Evans to Mr. Belmont, "Memorandum," June 14, 1962, from FBI File: Alcatraz Escape, Federal Bureau of Investigation, Washington, D.C.

Federal Bureau of Investigation. "Clarence Anglin, John William Anglin, and Alfred Anglin." [File Number 76-26295]. Records of the Federal Bureau of Investigation. National Archives and Records Administration, College Park, MD. Photocopy in possession of the author.

Federal Bureau of Investigation, Statement, n.d., posted at www.fbi.gov, retrieved August 1, 2024.

Florida Industrial School. Intake & Exit Ledger. Section 1945 & 1946. Series 1121. Florida State Archives, Tallahassee.

Inmate Interview at U.S. Penitentiary – Atlanta, February 28, 1964, Alcatraz Escape File, Federal Bureau of Investigation.

Interview with an inmate at Leon County Jail, November 18, 1963, included in "Report of San Francisco Field Office," February 19, 1964, from FBI File: Alcatraz Escape, Federal Bureau of Investigation, Washington, D.C.

Interview with Allen West, June 15, 1962, from FBI File: Alcatraz Escape, Federal Bureau of Investigation, Washington, D.C.

Interview with Anglin Family, January 26, 1964, Report of SAC San Francisco Field Office. February 19, 1964, from FBI File: Alcatraz Escape, Federal Bureau of Investigation, Washington, D.C.

Interview conducted at U.S. Penitentiary – Atlanta, June 26, 1963, File #AT 76-224, from FBI File: Alcatraz Escape. Federal Bureau of Investigation, Washington, D.C.

Interview with Funeral Director, Lewers and Shannon Funeral Home, Ruskin, Florida, January 26, 1964, Report of SAC San Francisco Field Office, February 19, 1964, From FBI file: Alcatraz Escape, Federal Bureau of Investigation. Washington, D.C.

Jackson County Clerk of Courts. "Deed Records." Marianna, Florida.

Legat, Rio de Janeiro to Director, FBI, January 20, 1965, from FBI file: Alcatraz Escape, Federal Bureau of Investigation, Washington, D.C.

Price, Frank. Teletype to Special Agent in Charge, June 12, 1962. Quoted in "Anglin Brothers Escape From Alcatraz Prison," City Experiences. Last modified December 1, 2023. Accessed August 1, 2024.

Report from Jay, included in Report of Special Agent, San Francisco Field Office, June 26, 1964, from FBI File: Alcatraz Escape, Federal Bureau of Investigation, Washington, D.C.

San Francisco Field Office, Report, October 10, 1962, pp. 80-82, from FBI File: Alcatraz Escape, Federal Bureau of Investigation, Washington, D.C.

Special Agent in Charge, Atlanta to SAC San Francisco, September 10, 1962, from FBI File: Alcatraz Escape, Federal Bureau of Investigation, Washington, D.C.

Special Agent in Charge, San Francisco Field Office, Report, April 15, 1964, from FBI File: Alcatraz Escape, Federal Bureau of Investigation, Washington, D.C.

Special Agent in Charge, San Francisco Field Office to Director FBI, September 13, 1962, from FBI File: Alcatraz Escape, Federal Bureau of Investigation, Washington D.C.

Special Agent in Charge, Mobile, Alabama, to Special Agent in Charge, Atlanta, Georgia, September 4, 1962, from FBI File: Alcatraz Escape, Federal Bureau of Investigation, Washington, D.C.

U.S. Engineer's Office, Sausalito, California. "Statement." June 12, 1962. From FBI File: Alcatraz Escape. FBI Records. Washington, D.C.

U.S. Marshals Service. Alcatraz Escape File. Washington, D.C.

Interviews

Anglin, Guy. Interview with author. February 21, 2018.

Beasley, John, Interview with author, September 9, 2018.

Cox, Dale, Interview with author, July 8, 2018.

Cox, Dale, Interview with author, January 30, 2024.

Cox, Dale, Interview with author, September 30, 2024.

Former students, Florida Industrial School and Dozier School for Boys, 1940s-1980s, Dozier School for Boys Files, D.R. Historic Preservation Archives.

Gilbert, Adair, Interview with author. March 3, 2018.

Hunter, David, Interview with author. February 1, 2018.

References

McDaniel, John P, Interview with author. December 15, 2018.
Oakley, Ben, Interview with author. June 6, 2018.
Smith, Clint, Interview with author. June 1, 2018.
Standland, Robert Earl, Interview with author. September 18, 2018.
Whitten, Eliott, Interview with author. March 3, 2018.
Valenza, Donald, Interview with author. November 2024.

Additional interviews were conducted with law enforcement sources in Alabama, Florida, Georgia, Oklahoma, Texas, Louisiana, Ohio, California, Virginia, Indiana, Montana, North Dakota, South Dakota, Idaho, Washington, D.C., and elsewhere, 1990-2024. Names are withheld per agreement with these individuals.

Multiple members of the Anglin family also spoke to us on condition of anonymity. We respect their request to withhold their names.

Newspapers and Television News Reports

Ada Evening News, December 19, 1937, p. 1.
Altus Times-Democrat, December 20, 1937, p. 1.
Birmingham News, January 18, 1958, Page 1.
Boston Record American, December 17, 1962.
Carswell, E.W., 'Not Since Civil War Has So Much Been Taken at Gunpoint in Marianna,' *Pensacola News-Journal*, April 14, 1963.
Cates, Charles, "Alfred Anglin Electrocuted Trying to Flee From Kilby," *The Montgomery Advertiser*, January 12, 1964, Page 1.
CBS San Franciso, https://www.cbsnews.com/sanfrancisco/news/investigator-says-1962-alcatraz-escapees-likely-survived/, published February 8, 2011, Retrieved September 9, 2024.
Charlotte News-Press, January 10, 1975, Page 1.
Cincinnati Enquirer, January 23, 1958, Page 5.
Cincinnati Enquirer, January 22, 1958, Page 4.
Cincinnati Enquirer, January 25, 1958, Page 5.
Cox, Dale, "Informant claims one of Alcatraz escapees is still alive," https://twoegg.blogspot.com/2014/06/informant-claims-one-of-alcatraz.html, retrieved September 1, 2024.
Dallas Morning News, December 17, 1937, Page 1.
Davis, Mark, "30 Years on Lam from Alcatraz?" *The Tampa Tribune*, January 20, 1991.

Dothan Eagle, March 10, 1958, Page 1.

Dothan Eagle, March 14, 1958, Page 1.

Dothan Eagle, March 16, 1958, Page 1.

Enid Morning News, April 14, 1940, Page 3.

Fletcher, Carlton, "Georgia nephew of famed prison escapees keeps their story alive decades later," *Albany Herald*, June 23, 2020, Updated May 18, 2022, accessed October 1, 2024, https://www.albanyherald.com/features/georgia-nephew-of-famed-prison-escapees-keeps-their-story-alive-decades-later/.

Humboldt Standard, June 13, 1962, Page 1.

Jackson County Floridan, April 10, 1963, Page 1.

Jackson County Floridan, April 11, 1963, Page 1.

Jasper, Paul, "Ingram Loses; Bank Robbery Probe Is Told," *Pensacola Journal*, November 27, 1963, pp. 1 & 5.

KPIX, "Letter Originally Written By 1962 Alcatraz Island Escapee Surfaces," CBS News Bay Area (KPIX), January 22, 2018, https://www.cbsnews.com/sanfrancisco/news/letter-allegedly-written-alcatraz-island-escapee-surfaces/ retrieved July 22, 2024.

Miami News-Record, December 27, 1937, Page 1.

Morning Examiner, April 13, 1940, Page 1.

The New York Times, June 9, 2012.

Okmulgee Daily Times, August 12, 1939, Page 3.

Omaha World Herald, December 18, 1962.

Pensacola News Journal coverage, January 14, 1963 – February 24, 1963.

Pensacola News Journal, January 24, 1963, Page 1.

Pensacola News Journal, February 24, 1963.

Pensacola News Journal coverage, February 25, 1963 – March 25, 1964.

Pensacola News Journal, September 27, 1963, Page 1.

Retchko, Robert, "Local Man Jailed, Another Sought In $1 Million Drug Plane Seizure," *Fort Lauderdale News*, August 6, 1975, Page 2A.

Sanford, Bob, "Bonds set in drug case," *Jackson County Floridan*, August 13, 1980, Page 1.

Sanford, Bob, "Etheridges Tell About Landing DC-6 Loaded With Marijuana," *Jackson County Floridan*, November 13, 1980, Page 1.

Thompson, Paul, "EXCLUSIVE: 'In all the years we were together he never talked about those men' - Widow of drug smuggler who claimed he ran into the Alcatraz escapees in Brazil says husband was a 'con artist'," *Daily Mail*, October 16, 2015.

San Francisco Daily Journal, December 24, 1990.

Tulsa Tribune, April 14, 1940, Page 8.

Various national newspapers, December 17, 1937.

Various newspaper articles describing law enforcement interactions with the Klan in the Wiregrass area, 1960-2024

References

Quintana, Sergio, "Alcatraz Ferry Rescues 10 Passengers from Sinking Boat in SF Bay," NBC Bay Area, published August 4, 2017, Updated August 5, 2017, Retrieved September 14, 2024.

Books and Research Papers

Alabama Department of Corrections. "History of the ADOC." Accessed September 16, 2024. https://doc.alabama.gov/history.aspx.

Cox, Dale. *Death at Dozier School*. Bascom, FL: Old Kitchen Books. 2014.

Esslinger, Michael, and David Widner. *Escaping Alcatraz: The Untold Story of the Greatest Prison Break in American History*. Lafayette, CA: Ocean View Publishing, 2023.

DeNevi, Don. *Riddle of the Rock*. New York: Prometheus Books, 1991.

"[Names Redacted]." "Comparison Analysis of Purported Anglin Photograph." July 17, 2024. Unpublished report commissioned by the authors. In the authors' possession.

National Park Service. "The Post on Alcatraces." National Park Service. Last modified December 2, 2019. Accessed September 1, 2024. https://www.nps.gov/alca/learn/historyculture/the-post-on-alcatraces.htm.

Pettinato, Tony. "Did Two Cons Escape from 'Escape-Proof' Alcatraz?" GenealogyBank (blog). December 16, 2016. Accessed November 4, 2024. https://blog.genealogybank.com/did-two-cons-escape-from-escape-proof-alcatraz.html.

Widner, Ken, and Mike Lynch. *Alcatraz: The Final Escape*. Lyons Press, 2024.

Wohlfelder, Peter. *Alcatraz: Escape to the Bahamas*. Updated edition. Bloomington, IN: AuthorHouse, 2017.

Other Books by Dale Cox

The Fort at Prospect Bluff
The British Post on the Apalachicola River & the Battle of Negro Fort
2020

The Scott Battle of 1817
First U.S. Defeat of the Seminole Wars
2019

Fowltown
Neamathla, Tutalosi Talofa, and the First Battle of the Seminole Wars
2017

Nicolls' Outpost
A War of 1812 Fort at Chattahoochee, Florida
2016

Fort Scott, Fort Hughes & Camp Recovery
2016

Fort Gaines, Georgia
2016

The Battle of Marianna, Florida
2011

The Battle of Natural Bridge, Florida
2010

The Battle of Massard Prairie, Arkansas
2008

Index

Adams
  Forrest, 16, 17, 19, 21
Aiken, South Carolina, 55
Alabama Bureau of Vital
  Statistics, 86
Alcatraz, 1, 2, 1, 2, 3, 27, 28,
  29, 30, 31, 32, 33, 35, 37, 38,
  39, 40, 41, 42, 43, 44, 45, 46,
  47, 49, 50, 51, 53, 54, 55, 57,
  58, 59, 60, 61, 63, 71, 77, 79,
  80, 81, 82, 83, 84, 88, 89, 90,
  91, 94, 97, 98, 99, 100, 101,
  102, 103, 104, 106, 108, 110,
  111, 115, 116, 117, 118, 119,
  120, 127, 159, 160, 161, 162,
  163
Alcatraz escape, 3
Alcatraz Escape, 37
Alcatraz Island, 2, 27, 28, 29,
  31, 32, 35, 44
Alexandria, Virginia, 121
Alford, Florida, 73, 74, 75
Angel Island, 2, 41, 42, 44, 46,
  47, 54, 108
Anglin
  Alfred, 1, 3, 5, 7, 11, 12, 13,
    14, 15, 16, 17, 18, 20, 21,
    22, 23, 24, 27, 59, 60, 62,
    69, 78, 79, 80, 81, 82, 83,
    84, 85, 87, 90, 99, 115,
    123, 161
  Clarence, 1, 2, 3, 4, 5, 7, 12,
    13, 15, 16, 17, 18, 20, 21,

    22, 23, 24, 27, 28, 30, 37,
    38, 43, 45, 46, 49, 51, 58,
    60, 70, 71, 77, 90, 91, 92,
    93, 95, 98, 99, 102, 103,
    104, 105, 106, 107, 108,
    110, 111, 112, 115, 116,
    117, 119, 120, 123, 125,
    126, *See*
  Guy, 3, 4, 110, 111, 112
  Janet, 14, 16
  John, 62, 120
  John W., 30
  John William, 1, 2, 5, 12, 13,
    14, 15, 17, 18, 21, 22, 23,
    24, 27, 30, 37, 43, 45, 49,
    51, 58, 60, 61, 69, 77, 78,
    79, 92, 93, 98, 102, 103,
    108, 110, 113, 115, 122,
    123, 124, 125, 126, 127
  John WIlliam, 3
  Robert, 60, 99, 124
  Robert, Jr., 60
Anglin Brothers, 1, 2, 3, 4, 5, 6,
  7, 8, 9, 11, 12, 13, 14, 16, 17,
  18, 19, 20, 21, 24, 27, 30, 35,
  38, 39, 45, 46, 51, 55, 58, 59,
  60, 63, 69, 77, 78, 79, 81, 83,
  87, 88, 89, 92, 93, 94, 96, 97,
  98, 100, 102, 103, 107, 108,
  109, 110, 112, 116, 120, 122,
  123, 124, 125, 127

Anglins Brothers, 8, 12, 14, 15, 17, 18, 19, 20, 21, 23, 24, 30, 38, 40, 42, 44, 45, 46, 47

Armstrong Circle Theater, 3

Asboth
Alexander, 71

Atlanta, Georgia, 16, 17, 18, 24, 27, 40, 41, 42, 49, 50, 51, 52, 53, 54, 57, 58, 59, 60, 62, 78, 79, 80, 82, 89, 159, 160

Auburndale, Florida, 3, 110, 111

Augusta, Georgia, 51, 55

Bainbridge, Georgia, 11, 23, 24

Baltimore, Maryland, 76

Bank of Columbia, VII, 1, 2, 5, 7, 8, 9, 10, 11, 13, 14, 17, 19, 21, 24, 30, 49, 60, 63, 69, 103, 116, 122

Bank of Jay, 60, 61, 62, 65, 67, 69, 72, 76, 78

Barker
"Doc", 29

Baxley
Hon. Keener, 17, 18, 19, 20, 21, 24

Beasley
John, 11

Beasley Pharmacy, 5

Birmingham Church Bombing, 103

Blackwell
Olin, 38, 39

Blountstown, Florida, 11, 12, 24, 69

Bowden
J. Earle, 62

Brazil, 89, 91, 92, 94, 95, 96, 97, 99, 100, 125

Brizzi
Fred, Jr., 92, 93, 94, 95, 96, 97, 98, 99, 100, 125

Brown
D.K., Jr., 64

Brundidge, Alabama 116

Bulger
"Whitey", 29

Caldwell
D.K., Jr., 65, 66
D.P., 65, 76

Cali Cartel, 97

California Democratic Committee, 28

California Highway Patrol, 42, 43

Capone
Al, 29

Caravan Restaurant, 74

Caribbean Sea, 95

Carol
Forsyth, 66

Carswell
E.W., 72, 77, 161

Cathy
Relative of Anglins (Last Name Withheld), 102, 103, 104, 105, 106, 107, 109, 110, 118

Century Elementary School, 63

Century, Florida, 63

Chattahoochee River, 3, 5, 11, 69, 95, 104

Cincinnati, Ohio, 13, 14, 15, 16, 161

Citizen State Bank, 71

Citizen's State Bank, 71, 77

Citizens State Bank, 69, 74, 75, 76, 78, 89

Close
  Harold, 76
  Karl H., 76
Cobb Memorial Hospital, 52
Cohen
  Mickey, 29
Cole
  Ted, 30, 31, 32, 33, 34, 35
College Park, Georgia, 51, 53
Colombia, 89, 95, 96, 97, 100
Colquitt, Georgia, 3
Columbia High School, 12
Columbia Historical Society, 2,
  6
Columbia, Alabama, 2, 5, 7,
  12, 13, 61, 63, 69, 74, 75, 77,
  97, 100
Columbia, South Carolina, 54
Commercial Carrier
  Corporation, 111
Cox
  Dale, 70, 71, 78, 89, 92, 101,
    102, 104, 105, 106, 107,
    108, 109, 112, 113, 116,
    117, 118, 119, 163
Crockett, Oklahoma, 33
Cushing, Oklahoma, 31
D.A. White
  Police Launch, 32
Dallas, Texas, 30, 31
DEA, 97
Decatur County, Georgia, 11
DeNevi
  Don, 108
Denver, Colorado, 34
Destin, Florida, 77
Donalsonville, Georgia, 3, 77,
  103

Dothan, Alabama, 7, 8, 12, 16,
  17, 18, 19, 20, 49, 50, 51, 54,
  55, 58, 60, 103, 162
Dozier School for Boys. *See*
  Florida Industrial School for
  Boys
Dyke
  Mike, 41, 42
Early County, Georgia, 5, 13,
  104
Eastwood
  Clint, 1, 101, 116
Englewood, Florida, 95
Escape from Alcatraz
  Duathlon, 47
Escobar
  Pablo, 96, 97
Etheridge
  Charles F., Sr., 96
Evans
  Robert Glenn, 95
Fairview, South Carolina, 54
FBI, 1, 5, 8, 9, 11, 12, 13, 14,
  15, 16, 23, 30, 34, 35, 37, 38,
  39, 40, 41, 42, 43, 44, 46, 47,
  48, 49, 50, 51, 52, 53, 54, 55,
  56, 57, 58, 59, 61, 62, 63, 64,
  67, 74, 76, 78, 79, 81, 82, 83,
  84, 85, 86, 87, 88, 89, 90, 91,
  92, 97, 99, 103, 104, 110,
  111, 123, 124, 159, 160
Federal Bureau of
  Investigation. *See* FBI, *See*
  FBI
Field
  Morton, 46
Fillmore
  Millard, 28
Find-A-Grave, 112

Florida Highway Patrol, 74
Florida Industrial School for
  Boys, 4, 69, 70, 71, 159, 160
Florida State Prison, 27, 59, 70
Fort Lauderdale, Florida, 95,
  162
Fort Mason, 32
Fort Myers, Florida, 90
Fort Point, 29, 32, 45, 46, 47
Fulton County, Georgia, 57
Georgia State Prison, 59
Gideon v. Wainwright, 15
Gilbert
  Dr. Adair, 5, 8, 10
Golden Gate, California, 32, 44
Graceville, Florida, 112
Grand Bahama Island, 90, 91
Green
  James, 6
Greenwood, Florida, 101, 102,
  104, 105, 107, 108, 109, 110,
  112, 116, 117, 118, 121, 124,
  127
Guadalajara, Mexico, 89, 90
Gulf of America/Gulf of
  Mexico, 95
Hadden
  Lamar, 12
Haines City, Florida, 90
Hamilton, Ohio, 13
Harrell
  Joe, 66
Haynes, Florida, 90
Henderson
  Oscar, 67
Herlihy
  Ed, 37
Herring
  James, 49

Hess Marine, 63
Hill
  Roy, 18
Hillsborough County, Florida,
  69
Hoover Insurance Company,
  64
Horse Creek, 56
Horse Creek Lake, 56
Houston County Jail, 55, 57
Houston County, Alabama, V,
  VII, 12, 13, 16, 17, 18, 19,
  20, 21, 24, 49, 50, 52, 53, 55,
  57, 58, 69
Humboldt County, California,
  43
Hunter
  David, 2, 8
Ingram
  L.J., 65, 66, 67, 76, 162
Jackson County, Florida, 3, 69,
  70, 73, 74, 76, 90, 96, 102,
  103, 104, 105, 106, 107, 108,
  109, 110, 112, 116, 162
Jacksonville, Florida, 64, 74,
  76
Jay, 116
Jay Oil and Gas Field, 60
Jay, Florida, 59, 60, 61, 62, 63,
  64, 65, 66, 67, 72, 74, 75, 76,
  77, 160
Johnson
  "Bump", 29
  Hon. Frank M., 16
Johnston
  James, 33
Jordantown, South Carolina, 56
Karpis
  "Creepy", 29

Kelly
  "Machine Gun", 29
Kilby Correctional Facility, 78,
  80, 81
Kilby Prison, 78, 79, 80, 81,
  82, 84, 85, 86, 87, 90
KKK, 103, 110
Ku Klux Klan. *See* KKK
Lakeland, Florida, 90
Langley Pond, 56
Langley, South Carolina, 51,
  54, 55, 56, 58
Lawhon
  E.A., 66
Leavenworth, Kansas, 27
Lewers and Shannon Funeral
  Home, 84, 159
Lill
  John, 23
Little Alcatraz Island, 44, 45
Louisiana State Penitentiary,
  30
Lynch
  Mike, 94, 99, 163
Lyons
  Frankie, 104
Malone
  Price W., 61, 62, 65, 66, 105
Marianna, Florida, 5, 67, 69,
  70, 71, 72, 73, 74, 75, 76, 77,
  78, 89, 101, 106, 107, 108,
  109, 110, 116, 161
Marin County, California, 42,
  43, 47, 54, 108
Martin
  H.K., 20
  James F., 20
McClendon
  Mac, 102, 106

McDaniel
  John P., 73, 74, 102, 108
McIntosh
  Helen Taylor, 14, 16
Medellin Cartel, 96
Merced County, California, 34
Mexico, 89, 90, 95, 96
Midland Country Club, 56
Miller
  Carl V., 121
Miller County, Georgia, 3, 5
Mitchell
  Henry Clay, 67
Mobile, Alabama, 55
Monterrey, Mexico, 90
Montgomery, Alabama, 16, 78,
  80, 84, 86
Morris
  Frank Lee, 1, 2, 27, 29, 30,
    35, 37, 38, 39, 42, 43, 44,
    45, 46, 49, 50, 51, 52, 53,
    55, 57, 58, 60, 62, 67, 69,
    72, 77, 78, 89, 90, 92, 102,
    103, 104, 105, 106, 115,
    116, 117, 120, 121, 123,
    125, 126, 127
Mt. Meigs, Alabama, 78, 80
Muskogee, Oklahoma, 33, 34
National Register of Historic
  Places, 6
Native American, 29
NBC, 102
New Orleans, Louisiana, 58,
  72, 104
Newspaper
  Albany Herald, 87
  Cincinnati Enquirer, 14
  Dothan Eagle, 19
  Jackson County Floridan, 74

Pensacola Journal, 65
Pensacola News Journal, 61,
  62, 63, 64, 77, 162
Nix
  Jimmy, 9
Nix's Grocery, 9
North Dakota, 120
Oakley
  Ben, 8, 9, 12
  Florrie, 5, 9, 10, 17, 21, 23
  Walter F., 9
  Walter F., Jr., 10, 11, 17, 21,
    22, 23
Pacific Ocean, 38
Panama City, Florida, 74, 77,
  101
Parker
  Darl Lee, 45
Paul Pry Rock, 45
Pensacola, Florida, 60, 61, 62,
  63, 64, 65, 67, 71, 72, 76, 77,
  161, 162
Phenix City, Alabama, 52, 57
Pinder
  Freddie, 91
Polk County, Florida, 3, 90
Prescott
  Charles S., 18
Presidio
  The, 29, 32, 46
Price
  Frank L., 39, 42, 160
Raccoon Strait, 47
Raiford, Florida, 27, 59
Reidsville, Georgia, 59
Richmond, California, 32, 33,
  35
Rio de Janeiro, Brazil, 91, 92,
  94, 160

Roanoke, Virginia, 76
Roe
  Ralph, 30, 31, 32, 33, 34, 35
Ruskin, Florida, 3, 82, 83, 84,
  95, 159
Rutherford
  J.A., 31
San Francisco Bay, 1, 2, 28, 31,
  33, 34, 35, 37, 38, 41, 44, 46,
  47, 77, 80, 88, 118
San Francisco Earthquake, 29
San Francisco Police
  Department, 120
San Francisco, California, 1, 2,
  28, 29, 30, 31, 32, 33, 34, 35,
  37, 38, 39, 41, 42, 43, 44, 46,
  47, 53, 54, 55, 63, 77, 79, 80,
  82, 84, 88, 89, 107, 108, 112,
  113, 118, 124, 159, 160
Sandusky
  Bowers, 72, 73, 74, 75
Santa Rosa County, Florida, 67
Sausalito, California, 44, 159
Savannah River, 51
Savannah, Georgia, 51, 54, 55
Scott
  John Paul, 45, 46, 47
Seminole County, Georgia, 3,
  5, 69, 104
Senn
  Althea, 85
Smith
  Clint, 6, 9
Sonoma County, California, 33
Sowhatchee Creek, 11, 13
Spanish influenza, 70
SS *Oliver Cutts*, 45
SS *Paul Pry*, 45
Standland

Robert Earl, 72, 73, 75, 78, 161
Sudlow Pond, 56
Sunset Memorial Gardens Cemetery, 56
Susquelana, California, 41
Tallahassee, Florida, 46, 77, 79, 80, 102
Tampa, Florida, 3, 12, 23, 24, 69, 70, 85, 106, 162
Taylor
 Fern, 14, 15
The Bahamas, 89, 90, 91, 97, 163
The Everglades, 97
The History Channel, 87, 92, 94
Thrift Department Store, 72
Treat Mountain, 95
Troy University, 5
Two Egg, Florida, 107
U.S. Army, 35
U.S. Army Corps of Engineers, 44
U.S. Bureau of Prisons, 17, 29, 34, 38, 39
U.S. Coast Guard, 32, 45, 97
U.S. Department of Justice, 85
U.S. Marine Corps, 110
U.S. Marshals Service, 91, 99, 102, 104, 110, 123
U.S. Supreme Court, 15
Underhill Gang, 30
United Merchants Clubhouse, 56

University of Florida, 106
University of South Florida, 3
Unsolved Mysteries
 Television Program, 102, 107, 117
Valenza
 Donald, 12
Vaught
 Hon. Edgar S., 30, 31
Wagner, South Carolina, 54
Walla Walla, Washington, 35
Warrenville, South Carolina, 55
Washington, D.C., 121
Watson
 Elmer, 34
West
 Allen, 38, 44, 53, 103, 159
 Mae, 40
White Chapel Funeral Home, 84
Whitten
 Elliott, 6
Widner
 David, 87, 90, 99, 163
 Ken, 88, 94, 99, 163
Wilkinson
 Fred T., 18
Williams
 C.L., 7, 8, 9, 17, 20, 21, 22, 23
WJHG-TV, 101
Wohlfelder
 Peter, 90, 91, 163
World War II, 95, 97

www.ingramcontent.com/pod-product-compliance
Lightning Source LLC
Chambersburg PA
CBHW070039100426
42740CB00013B/2730